COACHING

MINISTRY

TEAMS

OTHER BOOKS BY KENNETH O. GANGEL

Understanding Teaching

Beloved Physician

Leadership for Church Education

The Family First

So You Want to Be a Leader!

Between Christian Parent and Child

Competent to Lead

Twenty-four Ways to Improve Your Teaching

The Gospel and the Gay

You Can Be an Effective Sunday School Superintendent

Lessons in Leadership from the Bible

Building Leaders for Church Education

Thus Spake Qoheleth

Christian Education—Its History and Philosophy (coauthor)

Unwrap Your Spiritual Gifts

Toward a Harmony of Faith and Learning

Church Education Handbook

Building a Christian Family (coauthor)

Personal Growth Bible Studies:

- *Matthew 1–14*
- *Matthew 15–28*
- *Acts*
- *Romans 1–12*
- *Romans 13–Galatians*
- *1 and 2 Timothy and Titus*

The Christian Educator's Handbook on Teaching (coeditor)

Feeding and Leading

Key Words for the Christian Life

The Christian Educator's Handbook on Adult Education (coeditor)

Communication and Conflict Management in Churches and Christian Organizations (coauthor)

Volunteers for Today's Church (coauthor)

Accent of Truth Bible Study Series:

- *Learning to Be the Church*
- *Growing in Grace and Godliness*
- *Rejoicing in Faith and Freedom*

The Christian Educator's Handbook on Spiritual Formation (coeditor)

Your Family (coauthor)

Called to Teach

Team Leadership in Christian Ministry

The Christian Educator's Handbook on Family Life Education (coeditor)

Ministering to Today's Adults

Stories for Struggling Servants

COACHING

Leadership and Management

MINISTRY

in Christian Organizations

TEAMS

KENN GANGEL

CHARLES R. SWINDOLL, *General Editor*

ROY B. ZUCK, *Managing Editor*

WORD PUBLISHING

NASHVILLE

A Thomas Nelson Company

COACHING MINISTRY TEAMS
Swindoll Leadership Library

Unless otherwise indicated, Scripture quotations used in this book are from the *Holy Bible, New International Version* (NIV), copyright © 1973, 1978, 1984, International Bible Society. Used by permission of Zondervan Bible Publishers.

Scripture quotations marked AMP are from *The Amplified Bible.* Copyright © 1965, Zondervan Bible Publishers. Used by permission.

Scripture quotations marked KJV are from the *King James Version* of the Bible.

Scripture quotations marked NKJV are from the *New King James Version.* Copyright © 1979, 1980, 1982, Thomas Nelson, Inc., Publisher.

Scripture quotations marked TLB are from *The Living Bible.* Copyright © 1971, Tyndale House Publishers. Used by permission.

Published in association with Dallas Theological Seminary (DTS):

General Editor: Charles Swindoll
Managing Editor: Roy B. Zuck

The theological opinions expressed by the author are not necessarily the official position of Dallas Theological Seminary.

Library of Congress Cataloging-in-Publication Data

Gangel, Kenneth O.
Coaching Ministry Teams / by Kenneth O. Gangel
p. cm.—(Swindoll leadership library)
Includes bibliographical references.

ISBN 0-8499-1357-8

1. Church work   I. Title.   II. Series

2000   CIP

Printed in the United States of America

00 01 02 03 04 05 06 BVG 9 8 7 6 5 4 3 2

CONTENTS

101683

DEDICATION

To the faculty of Dallas Theological Seminary,
for fifteen years my colleagues and friends

FOREWORD

EVERYONE LOVES a winner. We cheer the team piling up victories and shun the squads who fail to produce winning numbers. Normally the players receive the accolades. Trophies, ribbons, medals, and money flow to the participant who wins on the athletic field. Those who fail to produce are sent packing. At least that's the way it used to be.

Today money may be more a motivating factor than mediocrity in determining whether a player stays or goes. In today's world of huge contracts and long-term deals, poor performers can stay while the head coach gets fired. Strange, isn't it? As long as a team is winning, things are great. But watch what happens when a team hits the skids.

Attendance drops, loyal fans grow unruly, even the hot dogs taste bland. Someone has to take the blame. You would think the fans would turn on the performers, the ones running the plays. Yet more often than not it's the head coach who takes the fall. Did you catch that shift in loyalties? When the team is winning, people say, "The players are great!" When the team is losing people complain, "We need a new head coach."

There's nothing like watching a group of individuals coalesce around a common cause. Who could forget the dynasty that head basketball coach John Wooden built at UCLA? The Dallas Cowboys under their long-time leader Tom Landry also come to mind. And what about the Green Bay Packers who followed the guidance and tutelage of Vince Lombardi? May I be bold enough to inquire about the team you're currently building?

I've made a life-long study of leadership. There are many names for the leader: shepherd, pastor, president, chairman, coach. All these are leaders who gather individuals around them to form a team. My long-time friend and colleague, Dr. Kenneth O. Gangel, has been doing this for years. Therefore he knows much about teamwork. In several different ministry positions he has built teams that functioned smoothly and effectively. What are the keys to team building? Dr. Gangel has insightfully answered that question in this volume.

If God has given you leadership gifts, I'm sure you've struggled at times with exactly *how* to lead. There are days when those of us who lead feel nothing can stop us from accomplishing our God-ordained goals. And yet, if you lead long enough, you'll encounter bumps in the road, times of dryness when you need others by your side to help summon your strength. Joshua ministered to Moses on occasion. David walked with Jonathan, and he needed his "mighty men."

None of us would question the thought that Jesus could have "gone it alone." There's no doubt He could have stood as a steer in the blizzard throughout His ministry, and at times He did. And yet the picture we most often see is one of Jesus leading the disciples. He coached His team. Our Lord and Master served publicly for only three and a half years, and yet His goal and vision continue strong two thousand years later. How did He do it? What strategy did He employ to execute such an astounding mission? What was it about His small band of followers that "turned the world upside down"?

The strategy our Lord employed, and the one Kenn Gangel advises in this volume, is to "team build." You can go farther and faster with a team. There's nothing more beautiful than watching a team that's fully functioning. Members know their assignments. Trust builds. Optimism and motivation flow as people are built up and encouraged.

Personally, I'll take a team over an individual any day. And by the time you finish reading this outstanding work, you will too.

—CHARLES R. SWINDOLL
General Editor

# PREFACE

LEIGHTON FORD tells the story of a ride through the streets of Bucharest, the capital of Romania, on a wet June afternoon. "At a traffic circle, police suddenly appeared, stopping all vehicles. Our driver turns to us and says, 'I think you are going to see our president come by; they are clearing the way.'"

"We peer out, trying to see this infamous character, Nicolai Ceausescu, the ruthless dictator who had executed thousands of his enemies and ruined Romania's economy. Half a block away, a motorcycle escort appears, followed by an official black limousine. And in the back of the car we can see a mass of black hair. Is it the president's wife with an enormous hairdo? Our driver begins to laugh. 'It's his dog!' The president's dog, with a chauffeur, a limousine, and a motorcycle escort? In a city where the people cannot buy meat and get a ration of two-thirds a tank of petrol per month? In the uprising of 1989, the Romanian dictator and his wife ended their lives before a firing squad, summarily executed by a people's court for their mis-leadership."[1]

Misleadership. Mismanagement. Scores of Christian organizations and churches have suffered because their leaders, well-intentioned but ill-prepared, practiced misleadership. Leaders need to relate to other people much as a coach relates to team members. But a head football coach doesn't play linebacker, and in larger schools or professional teams he doesn't even train linebackers. He simply makes sure the linebackers get the best possible training.

This is a book about coaching—but in a field far more important than football, basketball, or baseball. The chapters portray pastors and Christian leaders as influential models who develop teams and help those teams reach goals. I attempt to develop a strong biblical base for this philosophy of ministry, so battered and bantered through the years, yet now achieving recognition even in the highest secular realms.

The thrust of this book stands against the majority of leadership books available today in the evangelical market. It turns away from techniques, manipulation, control, and quantitative measures, and focuses on how coaches empower players to be a winning team. Theology provides the foundation for leadership philosophy and ministry process.

This book is not just an extended discussion of a philosophic position. It is a practical manual for use in churches and Christian organizations. It comes with the humble prayer that God will encourage all who read it.

ACKNOWLEDGMENTS

Warm gratitude goes to my wife, Betty, who has encouraged me in my writings and has read the manuscripts of most of them. I also extend deep appreciation to all the writers who have contributed to this field during the years I have been teaching and writing. And hearty thanks to my secretary, Kathy Howard, for handling the manuscript in such a professional manner.

CHAPTER 1

The Heart of a Champion: Leadership Attitudes

T HE IMAGE REMAINS branded in the minds and hearts of basketball fans everywhere. Michael Jordan, suffering from the flu, was struggling to keep his mind and body under control as he led the Chicago Bulls to the 1998 NBA title. His skills have never been challenged; most people consider him the greatest basketball player who ever lived. But his heart and spirit have probably won as many games as his jump shot. From his days as a college player at the University of North Carolina through that final series just before his retirement from the game, Michael Jordan played with the heart of a champion. This chapter is about the kind of attitudes and mind-set essential to coaching ministry teams. In churches, schools, mission boards, and parachurch organizations all around the world a new decade and century of leadership is just beginning. There are ministry teams forming on every continent and in almost every language, and all those "players" need solid coaching.

During the 1990s the United States boasted approximately 325,000 local congregations, nearly one church for every 550 adults, a better ratio than McDonalds, Sears, or the United States Postal Service. Americans tend to be a religious lot. Four out of five of us consider ourselves Christians, but only one out of five has any understanding of the gospel. With all the sociological analysis of church and culture available to us, one danger in modern Christian leadership seems to be the tendency to deemphasize the distinctives of Christianity in order to make it more palatable to the multitudes.

Since those 325,000 congregations are rarely more effective than the leaders who serve them, one of those distinctives centers in leadership or management patterns. Christians too often absorb the sociological assessment of the culture and then turn to a similar analysis of what kind of leadership will work in a given situation. Pragmatists that we are, we often do not stop to ask if it is right, or more important, if it is biblical. That failure can be destructive, perhaps even fatal, to a congregation. We see this dramatically illustrated in an interesting passage of Scripture not commonly utilized in managerial studies.

BIBLICAL BACKGROUND: JESUS

At that time Jesus said, "I praise you, Father, Lord of heaven and earth, because you have hidden these things from the wise and learned, and revealed them to little children. Yes, Father, for this was your good pleasure. All things have been committed to me by my Father. No one knows the Son except the Father, and no one knows the Father except the Son and those to whom the Son chooses to reveal him. Come to me, all you who are weary and burdened, and I will give you rest. Take my yoke upon you and learn from me, for I am gentle and humble in heart, and you will find rest for your souls. For my yoke is easy and my burden is light." (Matt. 11:25–30)

Often Jesus answered disciples' questions or responded to challenges from critics, but here He invited the disciples to look at Him closely and see what biblical leadership must be. As the text unfolds, we see Him calling both weary leaders and burdened leaders, struggling servants like the disciples, whose tendencies toward independence thwarted His efforts to help them.

Once He had their attention, Jesus pinpointed two distinct qualities of His leadership—gentleness and humility. We will come back to these later in the chapter, but here we notice that Christlike leadership must center in biblicism, not pragmatism; we must do what is right, not what experts tell us will work. Modern literature tells us that strong churches require strong leaders. The word "strong" seems to recommend an aggressive, autocratic leadership that takes charge and lets people know how

2

things must be done. We call this style *visionary* and *charismatic*, but it still comes down to their imperious behavior.

CULTURAL PERVERSION

Every two years politicians show us how the kings of the Gentiles behave. As we watch their televised campaigns, we are reminded again of Jesus' words to His disciples the night before the Crucifixion: "The kings of the Gentiles lord it over them; and those who exercise authority over them call themselves Benefactors. But you are not to be like that" (Luke 22:25–26). Servant leaders in positions of authority should do more than maintain certain attitudes; they should also display them, offering an incarnate worldview, a model of team leadership. Yet the concept of "managerial meekness" seems an oxymoron in the modern world. The cultural perversions we must overcome to achieve the biblical pattern are many, and here we mention three.

Inflated Self-Esteem

In Romans 12:3–8 Paul discussed the role of authority in the church. He had never seen the Roman congregation, but through the coaching of the Holy Spirit he wrote to them about leadership issues in that church. Here's a sample: "For by the grace given me I say to every one of you: Do not think of yourself more highly than you ought, but rather think of yourself with sober judgment, in accordance with the measure of faith God has given you" (12:3).

Four times in this verse Paul used various forms of the word *phroneō* ("to think"). The obvious play on words emphasizes the servant mentality of leadership so clearly defined by our Lord.

Christian leaders must be a special brand, coaches who think with sober judgment coupled with serving faith, both a gift from God.

Many believe meekness forces us to some kind of subordination in the leadership lineup, and in a real sense that is true. Servanthood is voluntary subordination, precisely what Jesus did with and for His disciples. But primarily meekness is a virtue in which Christian leaders measure themselves by God's standards. One attitude that keeps us from true biblical meekness is our childish insistence on always being right. We tend to take many church issues personally, as though all our worth is wrapped up in what we know and what we can do. Such a posture isolates us from the very people we must serve.

Persistent Autocracy

How interesting that even secular research has abandoned an antibiblical idea still clasped tightly by many evangelicals. When I first began studying leadership and management four decades ago, we saw only the first light of research suggesting that maybe Niccolò Machiavelli was wrong, that leadership works better with cooperation rather than control. Now the most cutting-edge management books constantly talk about leadership teams and denounce the persistent autocrat. William Drath writes, "In such a world, leadership is developed by developing the whole community of people so that they can participate more effectively in the relationships of leadership. As Joseph Rost has imagined it, people called *leaders* and people called *followers* are understood as being two sides of the same leadership coin, and we try to develop the coin itself—the whole interactive set of relationships comprising leadership. Thus 'leaders' and 'followers' all get 'leadership development training' and learn how to participate effectively in the process of leadership."[1]

Team leaders trust group decision-making, and they frequently consult with others. For years, critics have thrown stones at committees for their inept and ineffective behavior. We all know that the effectiveness of any group or committee depends on its leaders; but in my opinion, in a Christian organization any ponderous committee is far better than an oppressive managerial ego.

Abusive Power

Christian leaders must stand in stark contrast to mega-salaried executives who cut thousands of jobs to the applause of their stockholders. *Newsweek* called these late twentieth-century corporate bullies "the hit men." In early 1996 Robert Allen of AT&T laid off forty thousand people, while retaining his own salary of $3,362,000. While Edward Brennan was CEO at Sears, he drew a salary of $3,075,000 and was responsible for fifty thousand layoffs in January 1993. In August 1995 Walter Shipley at Chemical/Chase Manhattan laid off twelve thousand people and that year took home a salary of $2,496,154.[2]

The behavior of the world sometimes slips over into the church. Ron Enroth warns us about "churches that abuse," and one of the marks of such a congregation is "manipulation and control." He writes, "Spiritually abusive groups routinely use guilt, fear, and intimidation as effective means for controlling their members. In my opinion, the leaders consciously foster an unhealthy form of dependency, spiritually and interpersonally, by focusing on themes of submission, loyalty, and obedience to those in authority. In all totalitarian environments, dependency is necessary for subjugation."[3]

With all the emphasis on quantifying "healthy churches" many church leaders are focusing on numbers rather than on serving people to bring them closer to Christ. Too many church leaders have fallen into the trap of personal kingdom building, a focused concern on one's own and present ministry without a wider recognition of kingdom participation.

Of course, leaders must ask what is best for a given ministry at a given time, but we must not lose sight of the long-range target, the advancement of God's work. And lest we feel that personal significance or identity will be lost in such a vast enterprise, we dare not forget that servant leaders can be secure in their ministries because they know God values them. In any given ministry, team leaders convey this cooperative energy to each team member and the team as a whole. To quote William Drath again, "The learning organization will need a model of leadership that points toward continuous developmental and adaptive change. This suggests that somehow we have to figure out how to achieve flexible navigation instead of steady direction. It's an image of a ship on which interdependent sailors call out to one another what they are doing and what they have learned about the sea in which they are sailing."[4]

BIBLICAL SOLUTIONS

Matthew 12 deals with Sabbath controversies. Verses 1–14 speak to the issues of working and healing on the Sabbath. Then Matthew described

Jesus' additional confrontations with the Pharisees. Verses 18–21 form a paragraph that the editors of the New International Version have titled "God's chosen servant," in which Matthew described Jesus' healing ministry by linking it with the suffering servant motif of Isaiah 42. Presumably Matthew wanted his readers to understand the dramatic contrast between the religious leaders who attacked Jesus and the behavior of God's Son.

Ministry Appointment

Jesus presented a pattern for all those appointed by God to a ministry both distinctive and alien to the culture in which it must be carried out. As the Father's servant, He was chosen by God (Matt. 12:18), a reminder that a sense of calling is foundational to serving in leadership. John C. Maxwell wrote about the entry level of leadership, which he names *position*. "When a person gains authority through position, he lays hold of the title by rights. People follow him because they have to. Do not falsely assume when you are 'voted' into a church that you have earned the congregation's following and allegiance."[5] Maxwell then adds four other levels—*permission, production, personal development*, and *personhood*.

We also learn from Matthew 12:18 that God loves His chosen servant and delights in Him. We see that relationship in the way Jesus led the disciples. Vern Heidebrecht notes that there are three phases to the Lord's ministry with His disciples: He was with them, He sent them, and He gave them authority.[6] So we too struggle with difficulties in bad times, while fully aware that we are chosen by God, loved by Him, and delighted in by Him. Then as we develop disciples we seek to follow the same leadership formula the Lord used.

The third element in verse 18 reminds us that God's chosen servant was endowed with His Spirit. Henri Nouwen claims that many Christian leaders can't satisfactorily function as spiritual leaders because "most of them are used to thinking in terms of large-scale organizations, getting people together in churches, schools, and hospitals, and running the show as a circus director. They have become unfamiliar with, and even somewhat afraid of, the deep and significant movements of the Spirit."[7]

Ministry Assignment

Matthew 12:19–20 suggests five characteristics that ought *not* to be true of God's chosen servants. In other words biblical leaders should be marked primarily by their difference from the world around them, not by how well they measure up to its standards. First, *biblical leaders do not quarrel.* The Greek verb *erizō,* "to quarrel," appears only here in the New Testament, but Paul used the related noun *eritheia* five times in his epistles and James employed it twice.[8] In every case it carries the negative idea of contention. Interestingly, the New International Version translates it in Philippians 2:3 by the words "selfish ambition."

Perhaps the positive corollary of quarreling is *meekness.* We're reminded of Romans 12:3, "For by the grace given me I say to every one of you: Do not think of yourself more highly than you ought, but rather think of yourself with sober judgment, in accordance with the measure of faith God has given you." How did Jesus display meekness? By mingling with the poor, by putting up with the disciples, but especially by His conduct when on trial in Pilate's Hall.

Second, *biblical leaders do not cry out.* The Greek verb for "cry out" (*kraugazō*) means "to make noise" or "to scream." John used it in describing the screaming of murderous crowds at the Crucifixion (John 19:6). Christian leaders should not be loud, boisterous people whose public behavior brings shame to their ministry. Rather, they should function in dignity, a second positive quality that follows right along with meekness.

Third, *biblical leaders do not make a public spectacle of themselves.* Matthew 12:19 says, "No one will hear his voice in the streets." This is not a picture of silence, because the servant obviously proclaims justice and others hear him. But it does portray humility. In May 1991 *USA Today* published a list of what it called "The Ten Sleaziest Vocations in America." Number one was drug-pushing; number two, prostitution; and number three, television evangelism. We do not have to agree with this list to admit that ministry is more difficult in our time because some Christian leaders have made public spectacles of themselves.

Fourth, *biblical leaders are gentle* ("a bruised reed he will not break," 12:20). Consider this observation regarding communist leadership, written by Mihail

Heller: "The Communist system produces worship of the leader as a snake produces poison. The leader's authority embodies the wisdom of the Party . . . and is an inescapable and essential element of the system."[9] This philosophy was clearly articulated in 1919 by Vladimir Lenin. By contrast, we must be gracious and thoughtful toward those we serve.

Fifth, *biblical leaders are patient* ("a smoldering wick he will not snuff out," 12:20). We dare not advance our ministries and goals with impatience and callousness toward the weak and inarticulate, or forget that we serve them, not they us. But unfortunately Western society is not servant-friendly.

Ministry Achievement

Matthew then added that God's servant will lead justice to victory and the nations to hope (Matt. 12:20–21), obvious paraphrases of Isaiah 42:3–4. Isaiah referred here to the Lord's ultimate redemption of His people and His rule over the entire world. We dare not miss the practical application: The Lord's servant practices affirmation of other people. Our ministry must be so compassionate that even the weakest are not trampled but rather are offered justice and hope. For such a Messiah, Israel was hardly prepared. For such a church leader, twenty-first-century Americans are no more prepared.

Morton Rose reminds us that "affirmation is a servant leader's way of saying to followers how important their ministries are and giving a needed endorsement, providing support, and entering the celebration."[10] And one might add that that all should be done from a proper motivation of ministry and not to manipulate their continued involvement in *our* programs. Biblical leaders genuinely and seriously expect "greater things" from their teams (John 14:12).

Some years ago I attempted to pull together from the Scriptures fifteen dimensions of godly leadership, which, pooled together in a narrative paragraph, look like this:

> Biblical leadership takes place when divinely appointed men and women accept responsibility for obedience to God's call. They recognize the importance of preparation time, allowing the Holy Spirit to develop tenderness

of heart and skill of hands. They carry out their leadership roles with deep conviction of God's will, clear theological perspective from His Word, and an acute awareness of the contemporary issues which they and their followers face. Above all, they exercise leadership as servants and stewards, sharing authority with their followers and affirming that leadership is primarily ministry to others, modeling for others and mutual membership with others in Christ's body.[11]

How do we develop the heart of a champion, as seen in Matthew 12:18–21? Here are a few simple suggestions.

1. Ask the Holy Spirit to replace natural selfish ambition with a burning desire to serve others. We are, after all, sinful people.
2. Measure everything you read and hear about leadership by the standards of God's Word.
3. Determine (by God's grace) that the unbiblical leadership style of others will not unbalance your efforts to emulate the biblical pattern.
4. Acknowledge both in your heart and publicly that your achievements are the result of God's grace spread like a sheltering blanket over your life, your family, and your ministry.

PRACTICAL APPLICATION

The fascinating record of the servant of God in Matthew 12 tells us what a biblical Christian leader looks like. Today we talk about change agents, movers and shakers, people who can take control. But the servant of God, reflecting the Lord's own leadership style, practices restraint, not control. Jesus reversed what we might call "the law of the wolf pack," which had strangled Old Testament Judaism for centuries. As David Neer puts it, "Leadership is more than a person occupying a role; it is a process that can be shared. In all of its manifestations, liberation leadership is exceptionally important. It has the potential to free individuals and organizations. It can facilitate the learning that will help individuals break their co-dependence and allow them to apply their human spirit to their work. It can help build organizations that will thrive and grow through collective learning."[12]

The flaws in the monarchical system are not limited to the current British royal family, the madness of King George III, or the excesses of Henry VIII. Jealousy, intrigue, violence, envy, and political murder have marked monarchical leadership from the days of Saul. Only when Jesus sits on the throne of David in the Millennium will we see monarchical leadership (that is, His rule) work correctly.

But what can we do now in our own churches and organizations to practice meekness in ministry? Try these leadership exercises.

Reflect on Your Vocation

Take another look at your "appointment." What has God called you to do? How does one interpret "call" in the twenty-first century? Certainly there are times of loneliness and isolation, but they should be created by our closeness to the Lord, not our distance from other people because of exaggerated self-importance. As we think about Jesus washing the disciples' feet, it's difficult to imagine any modern Christian leader who has too drastically humbled himself or herself. Normally we see just the reverse.

Repair Your Relationships

I'm told that musicians always like to play Duke Ellington's charts. Almost everybody in the music business gives two "thumbs up" for what the Duke wrote or arranged. When asked why this was so, Ellington once responded, "You keep their weaknesses in mind as you write; that way you astonish them with their strengths." Team leaders focus on a relational high and keep self-centeredness on the lowest shelf.

A scene in the movie *First Knight* depicts King Arthur showing Sir Lancelot a small plaque on the round table. Embedded in the table is the plaque with the words, "In serving each other we become free."

Team leadership allows those of us in the body of Christ to stand together because we're willing to change in order to help others stand. As the old hymn puts it, "We are not divided; all one body we."

Refresh Your Body

During the years I spent as a student on a Christian college campus, it was fashionable to write in the back of one's Bible little mottoes offered by visiting speakers in chapel and other special events. One of the clichés that impressed me profoundly when I first heard it sounded something like this: "It is better to burn out for God than to rust out." With sophomoric sophistication I quickly grabbed my ballpoint pen, found an empty space amid the other "sanctified" graffiti, and wrote down this latest quotation, which I was doomed to live out too often during my own ministry.

As the maturing process wore on, I began to realize that such a two-option analysis of serving God was more motto than meaning, more trite than truth. Surely both of those extremes are undesirable. Certainly God's best plan for a Christian leader is to wear out faithfully and slowly during the years of active service.

Throughout those years God has often drawn me to the following passage from the ministry of our Lord. "While Jesus was in one of the towns, a man came along who was covered with leprosy. When he saw Jesus, he fell with his face to the ground and begged him, 'Lord, if you are willing, you can make me clean.' Jesus reached out his hand and touched the man. 'I am willing,' he said. 'Be clean!' And immediately the leprosy left him. Then Jesus ordered him, 'Don't tell anyone, but go, show yourself to the priest and offer the sacrifices that Moses commanded for your cleansing, as a testimony to them.' Yet the news about him spread all the more, so that crowds of people came to hear him and to be healed of their sicknesses. But Jesus often withdrew to lonely places and prayed" (Luke 5:12–16).

Ministry leadership is a high-tension profession wherever it is practiced, and the sheer schedule demands have placed responsible leaders in great demand—we belong to everybody. The pressures of leadership are certainly greater in number and different in type than forty years ago. But the greatest pressure does not differ much from that experienced two thousand years ago in Jesus' ministry—the pressure of people. "Crowds of people came to hear him and to be healed of their sickness." Who among us has not felt that everybody seems to want something from us, sometimes people we do not know and whose names we don't recognize?

Jesus tried to solve the problem of popularity and pressure by seeking privacy. He "often withdrew to lonely places and prayed." This was not monasticism; it was a genuine biblical desire for meditation and prayer. Maturity helps slow down the neurotic compulsion to duty. Mature people can work without playing and play without feeling they ought to be working.

Revitalize Your Friendships

Ministry leadership brings with it the need to talk to "safe" people, people who can empathize with our problems because they have experienced similar problems. Yet they must be people who can keep what we share in confidence. One could argue here for professional retreats, bringing together Christian leaders from different places to share their problems as well as their blessings. On such an occasion we share one another's burdens on a level of understanding probably impossible within any leader's own immediate sphere.

Refuel Your Spirit

Our Lord used His times of withdrawal to pray. The value of spiritual vacations as well as shorter days of meditation and prayer can be argued from His practice. How many times did Jesus feel the need to withdraw? Luke wrote that He did it *often*. How long did He stay in these remote places to pray? We don't know, but it is surely safe to argue that there ought to be a positive correlation between the intensity of schedule and the frequency of prayer and rest. Just as an air traffic controller needs more and longer periods of rest and relaxation than a landscape architect, so ministry leaders likely face greater needs for "refueling" than librarians or consultants.

Rethink Your Priorities

The workaholic syndrome must give way to the balance which this chapter has emphasized in order for leaders to survive and achieve the goals God wants them to achieve. Physical and mental refreshment are necessary on a daily basis where we may measure them in minutes, on a monthly basis where we may measure them in days, and a yearly basis in which we may measure them in weeks. Placing body, mind, and spirit close to the front follows Jesus' example and also makes good common sense. Champions calculate priorities carefully and understand that leadership begins by making good decisions about themselves.

As a summary of the last few paragraphs consider the words of John Greenleaf Whittier in an old hymn.

> Dear Lord and Father of mankind,
> Forgive our foolish ways!
> Reclothe us in our rightful minds;
> In purer lives Thy service find.
> In deeper reverence, praise.
>
> Drop Thy still dews of quietness,
> Till all our strivings cease;
> Take from our souls the strain and stress,
> And let our ordered lives confess
> The beauty of Thy peace.[13]

CHAPTER 2
Gifted Players—Gifted Coaches: Gifted Leadership

O N J A N U A R Y 6 , 1 9 9 6 , I was glued to the television set just before the opening of the Green Bay/San Francisco game at Candlestick Park. One of the cameras zoomed in on the Green Bay bench, shooting over the shoulders of that host of players who would not be taking to the field at the start of the game. Their captain, defensive end Reggie White, screamed over the crowd noise at his teammates: "Keep focused on the game. Don't you think about nothin' else. Be ready to play. Be ready to come in when we need you."

Green Bay won that game, and Reggie's point was critical: Team sports are won by team play. As we saw in chapter one, the New Testament makes it clear that that is precisely the pattern God expects in church leadership. But it is more than just a pattern; for thousands of pastors, associate staff members, and lay leaders, managerial leadership is the exercise of a spiritual gift. Paul's words to Timothy and Titus on elders' qualities exemplify the many New Testament didactic portions on leadership. Only when we analyze these passages in the light of New Testament models can we practice "a theology of management," which for Christian leaders should be more important than skills.

Of particular emphasis in this chapter is the New Testament teaching on two spiritual gifts, which also pinpoint the distinction between two functions, leadership and management. The words *management* and *administration* mean the same thing, but *leadership* is different. One can be either or both leader and administrator, but a term like "administrative management" is superfluous.

In Christian ministry this distinction becomes purely definitional. We want church leaders to be effective administrators and church administrators to be good leaders. Both are better than either, and both can be taught and trained. *Leadership* is by far the more popular term in our day, but pastors quickly learn that a disproportionate amount of their time must be spent on managerial activities. The sooner we learn that management is ministry, the more joyful each day can be.

BIBLICAL BACKGROUND: JAMES

In the early days of Jesus' ministry, His own half brothers were among His most outspoken critics. In unbelief they taunted Him, not unlike the Pharisees. The Lord's words regarding the disrepute of a prophet in his own country do not represent some generalized proverb; they reflect His own experience.

But something happened after His resurrection. We do not know exactly when or how, but James was converted and became the accepted leader of the Jerusalem church. He seems to play a lesser role in Acts because Luke did not focus on Jerusalem, but James did emerge in Acts 15 as a solid spokesman for the mother church. The events surrounding that particular church meeting dealt with legalism, always an effective arena for satanic attack. In A.D. 50 the spotlight centered on what Gentiles had to do to become Christians.

James, the brother of John, part of the inner circle of disciples in the Gospels, had been replaced by James, the Lord's brother, a relative newcomer to the church. Luke does not allow us to attach any office or title to his leadership, nor can we argue with the slightest bit of certainty that he had the gift of either leadership or administration.

Likely he chaired the meeting, but not to dominate the decision or issue pronouncements. He essentially summarized the opinions of the group, and we learn in Acts 15:22 that the apostles and elders "with the whole church" decided to send the message to Antioch.

Though he appears for just a fleeting moment in the pages of the New

Testament, James offers us a glimpse of gifted leadership: faithful in his own church, willing to stand by his convictions and yet not force other people to believe what he believed, and quite content to allow the entire group to have a role in the decision-making process. No wonder Paul referred to him as one of the pillars in the Jerusalem church (Gal. 2:9).

In reality the church business meeting recorded in Acts 15 forms a microcosm of a broader cross section of Christian ministry. As leaders, we represent the local church in actual business procedures, but we also represent the universal church in behavior and demonstration of unity. Every pastor sooner or later finds himself in a controversial meeting of some kind, trusting God's Spirit for wisdom at that moment. In times like that, giftedness in leadership and administration shows itself.

THE GIFTS AND THE BODY

It would seem that every Christian has at least one spiritual gift, and some have more. Perhaps the Lord of the church places multigifted persons into positions of leadership as pastors, evangelists, or teachers, and in other roles where such "clusters" of gifts are necessary.

Spiritual gifts are probably not ready-made abilities to perform, but rather capacities for service that must be developed. For example, Christians with the gift of teaching should apply themselves to training, reading, and practice to enable the Holy Spirit to produce competence in exercising that gift.

Resource of Gifts in the Body

Scripture emphasizes the corporate use of gifts. They are not given to "turn on" an individual, but to build up the total body. Though believers do not use their gifts only in a church building (not to be confused with the church body), the exercise of gifts and the ongoing ministry of the body of Christ seem inseparably related. Edification is the purpose, unity is the context, and love is the controlling principle or attitude for the proper exercise of spiritual gifts.

Can a Christian have any gift he or she wants? Not really. God's sovereignty decides because He knows the needs of the church. One thing is clear: *No gift signifies superior spirituality or a higher level of walk with God. Rather than seeking new gifts we should recognize, develop, and use the one(s) we have.*

Relevance of Gifts in the Body

Every believer belongs to the body of Christ, the church. We cannot separate our understanding of spiritual gifts from the content of 1 Corinthians 12. In Paul's closely drawn analogy of the human body he suggested that God gives the members of the spiritual body spiritual gifts for the good of the whole body. We cannot have spiritual gifts unless we are members of the body. Neither can we be believers and not be a part of the body described in 1 Corinthians 12.

Every member of the church has a ministry. Ministry (serving) is what spiritual gifts are all about. Four primary passages make this plain (Rom. 12:4–8; 1 Cor. 12:1–31; Eph. 4:7–16; 1 Pet. 4:10–11). The ministry of Christ's body becomes, in reality, the ministry of Christ.

Every member of the body needs every other member. "So we, numerous as we are, are one body in Christ, the Messiah, and individually we are parts one of another—mutually dependent on one another" (Rom. 12:5, AMP).

Every member has at least one spiritual gift. The Greek word *hekastō* appears in 1 Corinthians 12:7, 11 and is best translated "to each other." How different our churches would be if we expressed less awe at the multiple gifts of others and less criticism of how people use or do not use their spiritual gifts.

Regulating Gifts in the Body

No gift today brings new revelation in the New Testament sense. Though Revelation 22:17–21 primarily refers to the text of that book, the principle of a completed canon remains, and there is no biblical reason to conclude that God has given new revelation in our day (Deut. 4:2).

No gift is required of all believers or given to all. The significance of the sovereignty of the Holy Spirit in giving spiritual gifts is at stake here. If we can judge a Christian's spirituality by whether he or she has received a certain gift, we will soon divide ourselves into the "haves" and "have nots," precisely the problem of carnality in the Corinthian congregation.

No gift marks believers as uniquely spiritual or special. Where a New Testament gift was closely associated with an office, there was a distinction (the gift of pastoral ministry is an example), and the contribution that a spiritual gift makes to edifying the body of Christ seems to be the basic criterion by which to judge its quality. Who receives what gift to make what contribution to the church is the prerogative of the Holy Spirit alone, and our only proper response is to recognize how God's grace operates in the whole process.

All gifts serve the body of Christ, its upbuilding, and its ministry. When Paul talked about "the body," he usually meant the universal church. Of course, we experience the universal church through local churches in space and time relationships. The gift of evangelism may operate in the world, but it ultimately benefits the universal church. The gift of teaching may be exercised, for example, through Child Evangelism or a campus Bible class under the sponsorship of the Navigators or InterVarsity Christian Fellowship, but the body of Christ benefits.

All gifts represent supernatural levels of more common ministries. For example, every Christian is responsible to witness, but some have been given the gift of evangelism. Every Christian may teach in some way, but some have the gift of teaching. Every Christian can speak a word of comfort to his or her neighbor, but some have the gift of exhortation. Every Christian should participate in proportionate giving of his or her income, but some have the gift of giving.

Spiritual gifts are supernaturally given from a supernatural source and operate on supernatural power.

All gifts are to be exercised in humility, unity, and love. The unique location of 1 Corinthians 13 between chapters 12 and 14, which discuss spiritual gifts, highlights the necessity of love in the exercise of those gifts. No spiritual gift carries any merit if it is not exercised in love. In addition to the dynamic of 1 Corinthians 13, we repeat Peter's words: "Most important of all, continue to show deep love for each other, for love makes up for many of your faults" (1 Pet. 4:8, TLB).

All gifts are geared to personal ministry. To make it even more clear, one might say all gifts have to do with the way we serve people. We teach *people*; we help *people*; we lead *people*. Believers must recognize the mutuality of the body of Christ. A spiritual gift does not belong to its recipient; it is Christ's, and all the gifted become stewards.

THE GIFT OF ADMINISTRATION

Jethro, the Bible's first "management consultant," proposed that Moses reorganize the way he dealt with problems among his people. Jethro's suggestion placed emphasis on administrative principles such as span of control, definition of roles, decentralization, and delegation—to say nothing of the leadership development achieved by involving scores of others in the administrative process.

Biblical Foundations

The Greek word for administration is *kybernēsis*. It is related to the word *kybernētēs*, which means "helmsman" or "one who steers or pilots a ship." This second word is used in Acts 27:11 and Revelation 18:17 of pilots of ships, but the first word, which occurs in the New Testament only in 1 Corinthians 12:28, suggests one who, like a pilot, superintends and directs a ministry.

Church Officers

How closely we should associate this gift of administration with pastoral ministry is difficult to establish. Many theologians link our present form of pastoral management to the New Testament offices of *episkopos* ("overseer") and *presbyteros* ("elder"). This is fine.

But we need to remember that administration is primarily a gift, not a position that might arise out of a gift. While it certainly would be advantageous for all pastors to have the gift of management, there seems to be no solid biblical basis saying that God *requires* that gift for pastoral ministry. Yes, administration must be a part of orderly church life; but if pastors are not gifted and trained in this aspect of spiritual ministry, who takes care of it?

The answer surely rests in the fact that most spiritual gifts are not limited to professional staff members in our churches. Every Christian has a spiritual gift, and an elder, a deacon, or a Sunday school superintendent might well be gifted by the Holy Spirit for management ministry. I suggest that we would do well to look for evidence of this gift when electing people to these and similar offices.

Contemporary Examples

How can you tell if you have the gift of administration? One answer would be an understanding of *how others assess your work*. If you have been appointed or elected to be an elder, it may well be because your fellow Christians have sensed the gift of management in your life.

Another signal is the *joy or interest you have in managerial activity*. Many people detest administration, considering it pedantic, unnecessary, and sometimes even unspiritual. But people who truly have the gift find themselves drawn toward directing the tasks of other people; they discover a genuine spiritual enjoyment in exercising that spiritual gift.

Don't forget the *Holy Spirit's witness in your life*. As He gives us inner assurance that we are God's children, so He can make us aware of our spiritual gifts and can motivate us to develop and use them in His power.

THE GIFT OF LEADERSHIP

Most of us would consider leaders gifted people. But the distinct gift of leadership is quite different and is separate from the general idea of talent or skill. Here we'll take a brief look at how the gift of leadership relates to the gift of administration.

Biblical Foundations

The word *proistēmi*, particularly as it appears in Romans 12:8 ("if it [one's gift] is leadership, let him govern [*proistēmi*] diligently"), designates one who leads. *Proistēmi* appears eight times in Paul's writings, usually with an emphasis on personal leading of others and care for them. In 1 Timothy

3:4 Paul identified managing or ruling one's own house and family as a prerequisite for pastoral ministry.

With meekness, church leaders involve themselves in concert with other believers to engage in ministry. We see no isolation here. The smog of selfishness and supremacy must lift to make this mutual ministry a reality.[1]

Church Officers

Why does the term *layman* often carry negative connotations? If an explanation appears simplistic and elementary, we refer to it as being written in "lay language." The general impression of *layman* seems obvious—a person unable to do certain things.

However, this distortion is diametrically opposed to biblical church order. The genius of lay leadership inseparably relates to using the gifts of leadership and administration. Of course, not every occurrence of the word *proistēmi* refers to the gift of administration, just as no one would argue that every use of the Greek words for "teach" or "heal" refers to those spiritual gifts. But the link between leadership behavior at home and leadership responsibility in the church is unmistakable.

In the sphere of the church, God's delegated human authority is given to elders for the purpose of overseeing and pastoring or shepherding. This is the picture given by Peter. "To the elders among you, I appeal as a fellow elder, a witness of Christ's sufferings and one who also will share in the glory to be revealed: be shepherds of God's flock that is under your care, serving as overseers" (1 Peter 5:1–2). This same emphasis is found in Hebrews: "Obey your leaders and submit to their authority. They keep watch over you as men who must give an account. Obey them so that their work will be a joy, not a burden, for that would be of no advantage to you" (Heb. 13:17). This is a proper use of spiritual authority which provides for the authoritative teaching of sound doctrine.[2]

22

Contemporary Examples

Surely models of the gift of leadership present themselves in greater abundance than models of administration. We've already mentioned the example of James in a business meeting, and many leaders today have had a similar experience. But in addition to possessing this spiritual gift, we must also give attention to our demeanor and attitude, for these reflect our inner character. When others look to us for guidance, we must not use such occasion to dominate them.

The gift of leadership does not require a public assembly, since it obviously begins in one's own home. Leading with various age groups in a wide variety of ministry settings is very likely related to distinct call.

Three elements rise to prominence—gifts, call, and training, in that order. If God has called you to coach ministry teams, you may be sure that God has gifted you to do it and also that you need training for the job.

In the fall of 1998 the National Basketball Association put its season on hold, only to watch it stagger to a start a few months later. Media sources reported apathy among fans for the billion-dollar industry. Apparently the failure of team effort in the NBA has led to reduced scoring in recent years. Might we be tired of watching superstar performances in lieu of team effort?

The season for team ministry in the church won't be canceled until the Lord comes, so until that time, we play better as a team of gifted people, called and coached to carry out the Lord's work together.

CHAPTER 3
Designing the Playbook: Creative Administration

EVEN BEFORE THE 1999 NBA FINALS began, the eyes of the world were turned to a sport that captured the attention of America—Women's World Cup Soccer. As they took the field in each game, the team demonstrated enormous energy and courage, defeating opponent after opponent. And in striking contrast to the somewhat haphazard play in the NBA, the U. S. Women's World Cup team operated with clean efficiency and remarkable teamwork. Cameras were commonly trained on the field of course, but occasionally we'd get a glimpse of Coach Tony DiCicco on the sideline holding a clipboard. And we knew that those few pages contained some exacting plays that the women had executed over and over again in hundreds of practice sessions. When coaching ministry teams, designing the playbook takes much time and significant creativity.

A nationwide survey conducted by *Your Church* magazine discovered that 61 percent of pastors would spend less time in meetings if they could, 37 percent would spend less time mediating conflict, and 34 percent would spend less time counseling. If they could gain that time, they would spend it in evangelism (58 percent), personal devotions (66 percent), sermon preparation (73 percent), and prayer (75 percent).[1]

These findings are disturbing—particularly the indication of how pastors would spend more time and, we can assume, feel the need to do so. Certainly behavior that produces more evangelism, pastoral devotional time, sermon preparation, and prayer would be welcome in any church.

And it's not just a matter of time; job satisfaction (ministry contentment) is also a factor here. In the same piece of research John LaRue Jr., discovered that "pastors who are the most satisfied about their use of time viewed their work differently than those who are less satisfied." Those most satisfied, he observed,

- limit their work to less than the average of fifty-five hours per week (their workweek ranges between forty-five and fifty-five hours)
- have learned to accept the fact that the job will never be finished
- regularly take at least one full day off every week
- use all their vacation time (twenty-five days a year on average).[2]

Perhaps that's where this book comes in handy. With more specific focus, creative managerial process can help. Creative leaders help the organization and its people to be innovative while seeking to accomplish basic objectives and standards.

Creative people bring about something unusual—a new teaching method, staff training program, or ministry idea. Or perhaps a fresh challenge to the processes and functions of a church or ministry organization. Such thinking comes out of an imaginative mind sensitive to surroundings, open to new ideas, and characterized by independent and reflective ideation.

Creative people are dreamers, dissatisfied with the way things have been because there's always the hope they can be better. Such an attitude evokes the now famous line, "Leaders challenge the process." Like leadership, creativity is learned; it often comes down to a restructuring and reforming of ideas.

BIBLICAL BACKGROUND: JOSHUA

As the Book of Joshua opens, we immediately sense the end of an era—Moses had died. The forty years of wilderness wandering had come to a close, and it was a time to rethink old ideas and challenge familiar processes. Now God would select Joshua as the new leader. Joshua's years of preparation allowed him to enter his leadership role with the important quality of *patience*, a treasured companion of creativity in leadership.

Creative leadership demands *dependability*, but it also demands *dependence*: dependence on God and dependence on other people.

26

Joshua also had a *strong handle on the Word of God.* "Do not let this Book of the Law depart from your mouth; meditate on it day and night, so that you may be careful to do everything written in it. Then you will be prosperous and successful. Have I not commanded you? Be strong and courageous. Do not be terrified; do not be discouraged, for the LORD your God will be with you wherever you go" (Josh. 1:8–9).

Every coach God used in Bible times knew His word. Sometimes that word was directly spoken, as in the case of Abraham and Moses, but at other times it was written, and Joshua may have been the first biblical leader to make that transition. Amid the crushing responsibility of military management, Joshua constantly meditated on God's Word, aware that its message would lead to his "success."

CREATIVE RELATIONSHIPS

When we talk about creativity in relationships, it becomes entirely too easy to cross the line from motivation into manipulation. To avoid that, to guard against it constantly, we fall back on Jesus' pattern in Matthew 11:28–30. Here I want to develop further an idea mentioned in chapter one—biblical leaders are gentle. The absence of gentleness in much of Christian leadership today makes its presence almost a novelty. Creative relationships center in how we treat other people. What does gentle leadership look like when coaching ministry teams?

Gentle Coaches Are Redemptive

Three times in my career, in two different organizations, I have had to help people face moral problems. This may be the most difficult issue to deal with in Christian leadership. Often leaders react by wanting to cleanse the organization immediately of scandal or potential scandal, whatever the cost to the perpetrator (who may also be a victim). Perhaps on this point, more than any other, we stand justly accused by that horrible taunt, "The Christian army is the only military unit that shoots its own wounded." Standing against judgmental legalism we have the wonderful words of Reba Rambo's song,

See all the wounded, hear all their desperate cries for help,
Pleading for shelter and for peace.
Our comrades are suffering,
Come let us meet them at their need.
Don't let a wounded soldier die.

Obeying their orders, they fought on the front lines for our king,
Capturing the enemy's stronghold.
Weakened from battle, Satan crept in to steal their lives.
Don't let a wounded soldier die.

Come let us pour the oil, come let us bind the hurt.
Let's cover them with the blanket of His love.
Come let us break the bread, come let us give them rest,
Let's minister healing to them.
Don't let another wounded soldier die.[3]

Gentle Coaches Are Patient

Sometimes it takes people years to develop their gifts and employ them effectively in serving the Lord. But then, some of us can remember our own early struggles. Only recently have I been able to share my personal testimony in public and have done so in several Christian college chapels. In every case I conclude by telling students, "If God can use me, God can use anyone."

Another aspect of patience relates to the leadership styles of those around us. If we are serving on a church staff or in some followership role and we see unbiblical leadership behavior on the part of others, particularly the boss, we must not be thrown off stride in practicing servant-team leadership in our own areas of responsibilities.

Gentle Coaches Are Dignified

Every NCAA fan knows the behavioral differences between Bobby Knight (of Indiana University) and Mike Krzyzewski (of Duke University). Both are winners, but their demeanor puts them worlds apart. Biblical leaders avoid complaining and whining. The financial appeals and gimmicks of many of the so-called Christian leaders we see on television reveal that they lack dignity. Think again of Jesus in Pilate's Hall or Stephen before the crazed Jews who were about to stone him. Picture Paul before Festus, Felix, or Agrippa. Christian leaders practice dignity in all situations.

Gentle Coaches Are Humble

All achievements and plaudits come as a result of God's grace in our lives. We often hear athletes say after a big win, "Our team gave 110 percent today," "This game was televised around the world, and I had a real statement to make," or "Our team has been the best all season, and we proved it today." By contrast, how refreshing it is to watch a winner gracefully acknowledge the *other* team's efforts.

I think that kind of attitude can be coached. First we display it in ourselves, and then we ask God to help us develop humility in others.

CREATIVE PERSONAL DISCIPLINE

In a loose society full of permissive ideas, discipline has fallen into disrepair except in good teams. Yet one clarion call rings throughout the pages of Scripture and in the careers of victorious coaches: Great leaders, both Christian and non-Christian, have always been disciplined people. And disciplined people live within appropriate boundaries of behavior.

Christian discipline can be of three types: enforced or external discipline, such as we use with children and immature people; self-discipline, which primarily consists of adult attitudes and decisions; and Christlike discipline, based on spiritual surrender. The last of these certainly embodies self-discipline, but it goes beyond it in that such a leader becomes Christ-controlled. All Christian leaders must come to the place at which they take responsibility for personal discipline rather than always needing the encouragement and push of other people.

Of course, the word *discipline* closely relates to the word *discipleship*. Both connote a controlled life. Just as a person finally settles down with one person in marriage, so a Christian leader "settles" into the ministry to which God has called him or her. At times such a decision may push out other good things, much as the selection of a spouse pushes out other good people. Such a narrowing process, however, forms part of Christ-focused self-discipline.

Discipline also helps us understand that we are not clock-punchers on an eight-hour day. In full-time leadership responsibility, work may never be finished. Therefore we learn to schedule time for our families, time for refreshing recreational activities, and time for rest. When we recognize that ultimate discipline comes from above, and we submit to that discipline, we stand in a position of discipleship.

Can a few practical steps move us toward effective Christ-focused self-discipline? No simple formula, even if applied regularly, will produce this kind of mature attitude. But we can find guidelines toward progress in the disciplined life. Leaders who desire to deepen their discipline should pursue the following five tips.

Begin Now

It is never too early to regiment oneself into this kind of life. Those of us who are parents ought to coach our children toward disciplined living from the earliest days of their understanding.

Pattern Your Life after God's Word

Remember Moses, whose disciplined life required him to exercise self-restraint in listening to the Israelites' murmuring and complaining for forty years. Remember Joshua, who was able to say, even at the end of his lifetime of struggle, "As for me and my household, we will serve the LORD" (Josh. 24:15). Remember Daniel and his friends in Babylon, who renounced all possible political advantages when they refused to defile themselves with the king's meat (Dan. 1:8–20). And remember Paul, whose faithful missionary efforts took him into hard places again and again, causing him to renounce himself and to bring his body under subjection, so that he might practice Christlike self-discipline.

Commit Yourself to the Control of the Holy Spirit

The Holy Spirit desires to fill us (Eph. 5:18), that is, to have absolute control over our lives each day. This is not some elaborate ritual; it is a simple dependence on and commitment to His working in us.

Set Goals and Work toward Them

Don't be afraid to be a dreamer. Think big, but try to think within the will of God. When God gives you the green light on a certain project, do it with all your ability and His power.

Do Not Be a Quitter

An old coaching cliché claims that quitters never win and winners never quit. Like Jeremiah, feel the fire in your bones (Jer. 5:14; 20:9), thrusting you so strongly into Christian leadership that you will be unable to quit! Perhaps the key verse in the New Testament with respect to this kind of living is Luke 9:23: "Then he said to all, 'Anyone who wants to follow me must put aside his own desires and conveniences and carry his cross with him every day and keep close to me'" (TLB).

CREATIVE THINKING

A game of tic-tac-toe seems a childishly simple exercise. Yet in the theoretical five moves, this game can be played 15,120 different ways. Life is not so simple, but the exercise of leadership, particularly the process of thinking and decision-making, requires the logical properties of the human mind which we use in such a game. Everyone admits the importance of thinking, but not many people consider how it can be done effectively. We tend to accept the human mind as a functioning agent which will always be with us and can always be depended on to do its task. The science of cybernetics has taught us much about how the mind functions by studying the mechanical reproductions of the mind in the form of computers.

Put Your Mind to Work

In leadership we talk about problem-solving and decision-making. "Problem-oriented" leaders (see chapter 4) tend to view the task of thinking through a problem as difficult and boring. Because of this initial negative mind-set, they shy away from the apparent difficulties inherent in thinking.

The basic nature of a problem presents certain alternatives. From these it becomes necessary to sort out possible solutions and follow through on a feasibility evaluation toward the solving of the problem. Our failure to tolerate the difficulty of deferred judgment often forces us to make early (and thus unwise) decisions.

Jean Buridan, a fourteenth-century philosopher, spoke often of a certain donkey with high intelligence but a low capacity for toleration of decisions. When placed midway between two equally attractive bundles of hay, he died of starvation because he could not find a valid reason to choose one or the other. The opposite extreme finds us trying to make one simplified solution fit every problem. Then we become more like Procrustes, who in Greek mythology had only one bed. When a guest was too short for the bed, Procrustes merely stretched his legs. If the guest was too tall, Procrustes accommodated the situation by chopping off enough of his legs to make him fit.

Failure to reach for as much information as we can possibly grasp tempts us to quit too soon. Hero of Alexandria, a mathematician and inventor, reportedly used steam in 100 B.C. to operate a toy. We can shrug off his experience as an idea before its time; but what might have happened if Hero had asked some crucial questions about the thought process of his explorations? Can steam be of any use in anything but this toy? How might a person possibly propel himself by means of this power? Could this force be produced on a larger scale? Necessity may very well be the mother of invention, but somewhere in the gestation period the process of data-gathering and deferred judgment makes possible the "natural birth" of a workable solution. And, to continue this analogy, objective decision-making may be likened to a midwife who helps bring about such a solution.

Understand Yourself

Know your own personality dynamics. Are you primarily optimistic or pessimistic? Will your thinking be open-minded or will it tend to be limited and narrow? Do you have the patience to cope with deferred judgment, or do you feel that you must rush in to solve a problem with whatever information you have? Think through attitudes that may color your mental process and thereby your personal and professional decisions.

Learn to Process Ideas

Too much of our technique in decision-making falls into the vertical pattern. We like to move in a stepwise process toward a certain goal. The information must be correct at every step, and we select and deal with only the relevant data. Such is the traditional pattern of decision-making. Creative leaders think *conceptually*; we often call it "seeing the big picture." Howard Hendricks writes that an essential element in creative thinking is "the willingness to be consciously intentional in our approach to an assignment. This purposeful way of thinking is conscious and deliberate in contrast to blind, undisciplined, and scattered thoughts. It involves the calculated development of creative behavior and human potential."[4]

Practice Creativity

Consider the following five axioms which can help you become a better leader by becoming a better thinker.
1. Practice the process of data-gathering, always attempting to get as many facts from as many sources as possible before making a decision.
2. Practice deferred judgment, waiting to make your decision until adequate evidence is available.
3. Practice lateral thinking by not always trying to walk in a straight line from your problem to possible solutions but rather by brainstorming unusual approaches to the problem.
4. Practice the "work aspects" of thinking in the expectation that you *can* become a more creative and positive thinker.

5. Practice creative thinking by projecting an unusual combination of uses for ordinary materials or ideas.

Creative administration is a way to reorganize your life and ministry to make more time for the things that really count. But let's not confuse it with a quick fix. And let's not confuse it with unleashing radical ideas on an unsuspecting congregation. When you're tempted to do that, remember Tom Wolfe. Not long ago he left the ministry—permanently. Things had been going reasonably well for the first three years, but wrinkles began to appear in relationships with lay leaders after Tom completed a doctor of ministry course, "Pastoral Leadership and Change in an Age of New Paradigms."

Tom returned to his church determined to take charge of the future—both his and the church's. He intended to "de-layer the hierarchy," reorganize the stodgy boards and committees he had inherited, and lead the church into new transformational behaviors.

How excited he was. How pure his motives. How bright the horizon would be when the parishioners grasped his vision for a contemporary, seeker-friendly, church-growth-oriented, healthy church for the twenty-first century.

Tom's class had taught him exhilarating new ideas and introduced him to models of functioning congregations that had achieved all these things. Surely it would work at his church; surely everyone, or a least almost everyone, would see the wisdom of change.

But Tom carried home with him a problem no one had diagnosed or forewarned him of, a virus that would soon infect the lay leadership like a deadly disease. Somehow he had ingested the idea that he was the leader, and unless he rode like Napoleon at the front of the army or stood Pattonesque in front of a giant flag, creative leadership could not occur. That heresy built his ministerial coffin.

No one had called him back to Scripture. And during all the psychological and sociological analyses of Christian leadership that were drummed into him in that course, no one had told him that spiritual and ministerial renewal in his congregation would be impossible without the biblical demands for team leadership, a style taught by Jesus and modeled by church leaders throughout the Book of Acts.

In fact, the congregation was so shocked by his new behavior, they hardly knew how to respond. They felt like a small town with a new sheriff intent on single-handedly changing the laws. Some opposed him openly; some left the church; some languished in expectation of better things ahead. But none felt drawn to cohesion or cooperation—it was Tom's church, to win or to lose—and he lost it within a year. Now Tom is out of the ministry—permanently.

Not because of flawed theology.

Not because of immorality.

Not because of incompetence in pastoral duties.

Not because of homiletical ignorance.

Tom is out of the ministry because he failed to understand and practice a biblical leadership style that could have pulled that congregation into a tightly knit collection of teams creatively headed toward common goals.

The story is fictional—but then again, it is not. Such ministerial calamities have occurred with disturbing frequency during the past two decades and, I fear, will continue with increasing frequency so long as evangelical leaders, particularly in local churches, place their faith in sociological paradigms rather than scriptural principles.

While boating on Schroon Lake in upper New York, Dawson Trotman, founder and president of the Navigators, heard the screams of a drowning girl. A strong swimmer, he dove in and held the girl up to his companion in the boat, who pulled her to safety. Turning back to grab Dawson, however, the friend could find no sign of him. He was under the water, perhaps already dead.

Time magazine put the picture of this Christian team leader on its cover with the caption, "Always holding someone up." With all the talk today about empowering others and sharing leadership, what better plaque for your wall, what better epitaph for your tombstone. If you and I are to serve God effectively in the new century, it will be because we have learned to be people who always hold someone up. That's what creative leaders do.

CHAPTER 4
Setting the Standard for the Team:
Leadership Modeling

E VERYONE KNOWS that what leaders *are* is more important than what leaders *do*. But that can become more cliché than reality. To be sure, attitude precedes act, heart precedes hands. But one's nature is examined and explained by one's behavior, and so leaders consciously or subconsciously model all the time—much like parents.

Here are some of the ways leaders behave and model: relate, organize, achieve, think, envision, and endure. And as we do these things in churches and Christian organizations, we set the standard for the team by modeling biblical leadership.

Modeling for whom? In a broad sense we are models to anyone who observes us over time. In a more intentional sense, however, we model for those whose developing leadership can be influenced by ours. The Denver Broncos won the Super Bowl again in 1999. As they showed their strength, almost every sportscaster who covered the team that year remarked on its multiple team leaders who modeled for other players what a professional football player should be.

So the scope of this chapter aims at two targets—your own leadership and the influence you have in coaching other leaders. I've always made it a point through the years intentionally to select and train someone who could be my successor. In almost every case that decision was outside the bounds of my authority, but it seemed necessary to have someone ready if the Lord and the board chose that person. Obviously the example of Moses comes to mind here.

BIBLICAL BACKGROUND: MOSES

For years Israel had lived in the shadow of the Apis bull worship of Egypt, and even after the Exodus that heresy still festered in their national system. The prayer of Moses recorded in Exodus 33 took place in the shadow of the golden-calf episode, between the breaking of the first tablets and God's giving of the second set. Despite the worldliness of Israel, Moses had developed a deep personal relationship with the Lord. "The LORD would speak to Moses face to face, as a man speaks with his friend" (Exod. 33:11).

Confirmation of Ministry

"Moses said to the LORD, 'You have been telling me, "Lead these people," but you have not let me know whom you will send with me. You have said, "I know you by name and you have found favor with me." If you are pleased with me, teach me your ways so I may know you and continue to find favor with you. Remember that this nation is your people.' The LORD replied, 'My Presence will go with you, and I will give you rest'" (Exod. 33:12–14).

Moses seemed on shaky ground after the golden-calf experience. The people had let him down, and Aaron had let him down. Like many twenty-first-century Christian leaders, he felt discouraged and defeated, in no condition to model ministry. Moses needed confirmation of God's plan. Moses told God that he knew the people he led really belonged to Him and not to any earthly leader.

So in reviewing confirmation of God's plan Moses also received confirmation of God's pleasure and of His people. As God listened to one man pray, thousands were blessed. Moses knew he belonged to the Lord, and he wanted to be taught God's ways more perfectly so that he could lead God's people more effectively. Why do we Christian leaders today forget that the people we serve really belong to God? How can we forget that He wants their well-being and desires their good much more than we do?

Credibility in Ministry

"Then Moses said to him, 'If your Presence does not go with us, do not send us up from here. How will anyone know that you are pleased with me and with your people unless you go with us? What else will distinguish me and your people from all the other people on the face of the earth?' And the LORD said to Moses, 'I will do the very thing you have asked, because I am pleased with you and I know you by name'" (Exod. 33:15–17).

Moses still seemed a bit unsure that God would follow through and go with them across the desert and into the Promised Land. He wanted to know how God's people were different from others. What distinguished them from the pagan nations they would encounter along the way?

What distinguishes Christians today? Must they dress differently? Speak differently? Perhaps in some cases, but primarily we work among people with different hearts—hearts that have been changed by the presence of God. God first emphasizes His *presence* and then His *promise:* "I will do the very thing you have asked, because I am pleased with you and I know you by name."

Notice how affirming God was when Moses needed affirmation. The Lord could have scolded His servant, and He did so on several occasions. He could have even punished Moses. But when affirmation was necessary so the work could go on, God stood ready to speak encouragement to His servant. How do we establish credibility? How do the people we lead gain credibility? Because His presence, now available through the sustaining power of the Holy Spirit, accompanies us daily.

Confidence for Ministry

"Then Moses said, 'Now show me your glory.' And the LORD said, 'I will cause all my goodness to pass in front of you, and I will proclaim my name, the LORD, in your presence. I will have mercy on whom I will have mercy, and I will have compassion on whom I will have compassion. But,' he said, 'you cannot see my face, for no one may see me and live.' Then the LORD said, 'There is a place near me where you may stand on a rock. When my glory passes by, I will put you in a cleft in the rock and cover you with my hand until I have passed by. Then I will remove my hand and you will see my back; but my face must not be seen'" (Exod. 33:18–23).

Up to this point Moses had done most of the talking and God had provided short answers to his requests. Now the pattern changed. Moses offered a five-word appeal—"Now show me your glory." This is similar perhaps to Philip, who, after walking closely with the Lord for three and a half years, still wanted to see evidence of His authority by having a glimpse of the Father (John 14:8). Moses' speaking "face to face" with God does not contradict the fact that Moses was not allowed to see His face. The phrase "face to face" is a figurative expression suggesting openness and friendship (Num. 12:8; Deut. 34:10).

Moses had a personal relationship with God, but even that was now enhanced. In proclaiming His name to Moses, God was revealing His character and goodness. God placed him into that now-poetic "cleft in the rock" (Exod. 33:22) and covered him until He passed by. We don't know what Moses actually saw, but we do know that this new and deeper revelation of God's glory was intended to develop much-needed confidence in this faithful servant. Moses had experienced the *presence* of God and reviewed the *promise* of God—but now he observed the *power* of God.

How important for us to see all three, to know that God is always with us, even in the tough times. Loneliness and discouragement can dissipate when Christian leaders recognize the presence of God in their lives. But sometimes He seems far off. So we must then fall back on His promise. What He said to Moses, He says to us: "I will do the very thing you have asked" (33:17). Awareness of these two things leads us then to focus on God's power. Power for salvation, yes, but also power for service. People who watch us will sense our confidence that the Lord can empower us.

What processes or techniques will enhance ministry modeling? Consider three: a scriptural strategy, a clear call, and determined discipling.

SCRIPTURAL STRATEGY

If you were to visit my study and sit across from the desk in the visitor's chair, you might notice a small piece of paper attached to the lamp. Since the card is blank on your side you might guess that it is a business card. But it has on it a Bible verse, which I adopted many years ago as my life verse.

Tucked away in Paul's final speech to the Ephesian elders delivered at Miletus, this verse concludes the first segment of that address dealing with Paul's personal testimony. The central idea goes immediately to motive—*why we do what we do*. And in the typical countercultural tone of Scripture, Paul affirmed that effectiveness in Christian life and ministry cannot be calculated by time, money, visibility, or influence. These are amounts—the cultural quantities of worldly success. For decades I have found in this one verse a compelling and propelling impetus to carry out what God wants me to do. "However, I consider my life worth nothing to me, if only I may finish the race and complete the task the Lord Jesus has given me—the task of testifying to the gospel of God's grace" (Acts 20:24).

Find the Priorities

Effectiveness in any ministry requires us to ask, "Why has God called me here and what does He want me to do?" Yes, it is possible to lose perspective of the forest by gazing at one tree, but we can also lose focus on that tree and get lost in the forest. That often happens to students in college, particularly in their first year. Finding priorities is not an act of selfishness or ego, but an answer to the question, "What does God want from me?"

According to Acts 20:24 Paul said, "None of these things move me" (NKJV). Paul referred here to negative things that failed to disturb him—fear of the unknown, the warnings of the Holy Spirit about danger, prison cells, and hardships that lay ahead (20:22–23). People today are "moved" or motivated by talent, money, love for sports, an obsession with achievement. These are all good things, gifts of God that should make us thankful rather than proud.

But Paul refused to be deterred by negative elements. Instead he expressed total abandonment to the will of God.

When Jesus told Peter that the apostle would die a prisoner, Peter turned his attention to John and asked the Lord, "What will this man do?" Jesus' answer might be paraphrased, "What I do with John is none of your business; you follow Me." That is the kind of priority we ought to model.

Recently the Pittsburgh Steelers football team has headed for the playoffs almost every year. A story floating around that city describes head coach Bill Cowher's priorities as family and football. People say he is so focused that one afternoon he was seated next to a woman at a civic luncheon and politely asked, "What is it you do?" The woman responded, "I'm the mayor of Pittsburgh." He was so focused on his priorities that he didn't even recognize who she was. We too need to focus on priorities in building an effective ministry team.

Finish the Job

Whenever I hear or use the word "finish" in the context of ministry, it reminds me of the Lord's prayer in John 17 in which He said to the Father, "I have brought you glory on earth by completing the work you gave me to do" (17:4). In a few more hours He would cry from the cross, "It is finished" (19:30). With that model before us, why do so many Christians start well and finish poorly?

We could talk about people who agree to teach a Sunday-school class or work with a youth group only to tell the superintendent or pastor a few weeks later, "I quit." Or we could look at colleges and universities, packed every fall with record enrollments, but with more than half of the entering freshman never completing work where they start it. Twenty percent of them transfer and graduate from other institutions, and 40 percent never finish anywhere. Unfortunately many doctoral students never finish their dissertation and therefore do not receive a doctor's degree.

John Mark, a young man who traveled with Paul and Barnabas, left the first missionary team (Acts 13:5; 15:36–38) perhaps because he was unwilling to submit to authority or refused to be disciplined or could not muster enough courage. It takes discipline and courage to finish. Not just to win, but to finish.

In the 1992 Olympics in Barcelona Derrick Redman was favored in the 400 meters. During a final time trial, he pulled a hamstring and fell to the track—out of the race. He rose, hopped on one leg, pushing away trainers and coaches who tried to help him. Seconds later a middle-aged man jumped out of the crowd wearing a Nike cap with the caption "Just Do It." Redman's father helped him hop to the finish line on one leg saying, "We started this thing together: We'll finish this thing together."

Ministry models finish. Whether quitters never win, I do not know. But in ministry leadership, winners never quit.

Focus the Message

I came to Acts 20:24 as a life verse many years ago because of its emphasis on grace. If restricted to one theme in all my ministry, I would want it to be the grace of God. Not just saving grace, but living grace as well. God has showered so much grace on my life I find it impossible to treat people with a rigid legalism.

As we think about modeling standards, we recall almost instantly that effective living and leadership require both strategy and mission. They are lost without each other. To put it simply, leadership means having a goal and knowing how to get there.

Paul focused on the message of grace because he knew messages can be lost or become hopelessly blurred. In the Middle Ages, the church lost sight of the gospel of grace in the trappings of medieval hierarchy. As the 1800s gave way to the 1900s, many major denominations lost their focus on the Cross, Christ's deity and bodily resurrection, and other essential doctrines.

In 1972 our family was clamming at dusk on the beach of Thetis Island just off the coast of British Columbia. Intent on bending and bucketing our prizes, we had piled our belongings in the sand and concentrated on our task—with our backs to the ocean. Quickly and quietly the tide came in and covered not only our shirts, towels, and shoes, but also a camera that never again worked properly. As amateurs we did not know you never turn your back on the ocean. As leaders we dare never turn our backs on the Cross or on God's grace.

I never tire of hearing how the gospel came to Korea. In 1886 a Welsh missionary in China, Robert J. Thomas, learned that the Korean language was somewhat similar to Chinese. He wondered whether the Koreans might be able to read the literature he was using in China, so he boarded an American ship called the *General Sherman* and sailed for Pyong Yang harbor. As the ship approached shore, conflict broke out between the Koreans and the American crew on the *General Sherman,* and the ship was burned. Every person on board died in that vicious battle except Robert Thomas, who staggered up on shore, his arms filled with Bibles and other pieces of gospel literature. He dumped them on the sand as the Koreans clubbed him to death. But the gospel had reached Korea, and today approximately 30 percent of the people of South Korea are Christians.

To coach well, we need a mission and a strategy. We must find the priorities, finish the job, and focus on the message. At the end of his life Paul wrote, "I have fought the good fight, I have finished the race, I have kept the faith" (2 Tim. 4:7). May we too finish well, as Paul did.

CLEAR CALL

The question haunted me in the final months of my seminary education and throughout most of the following summer. With a newborn son (our first child) arriving just weeks before commencement and being a part-time assistant pastor, I threw open the boundaries of my future ministry plans as Betty and I made lists of where God might send us—and why. At the top of the list was a return to southern Germany where I had spent some summer missionary service when I was in college. Another of several other viable ministry options was the pastorate.

Not on the list and never in our minds was the ministry of teaching full-time in a Christian college. Nevertheless in God's surprising sovereignty by the first of September we had pulled a small U-Haul containing all our belongings to Kansas City. Sometimes I still shake my head in bewilderment. Ever since my college sophomore year I had sensed God's call to ministry, but I was surprised that He had led me to a ministry of teaching and academic administration.

How does one get a handle on such a crucial question as this? How does one interpret "call" in these confusing days?

Call to Ministry

In the first half of this century Christians had little difficulty understanding "ministry." It meant serving as a pastor or a missionary, with some possible exceptions for people who served on staffs of larger churches or

44

participated in some of the fledgling parachurch ministries just beginning in that era.

Over the next quarter century (1950–1975) ministries like Christian education, radio, and college/seminary teaching came into focus. College and seminary teaching had been going on for decades, but the Bible college/Christian liberal arts college movement, as we know it, is not much more than one hundred years old. One could safely say that before the end of World War II, people did not necessarily view professors in those classrooms as "ministers." Obviously the twenty-five years after World War II also demonstrated phenomenal growth of parachurch ministries.

These ministries continue in the twenty-first century, but in addition other creative and exciting options must also be legitimately considered "ministry." One need not look far to see them. Hundreds of churches have designed ministry strategies aimed at crosscultural evangelism, children's ministry, media outreach, church planting, drama, and urban service. How we should rejoice to serve God in such contexts! In my college days the suggestion that "urban ministry" or "media arts" were legitimate ministries would have been laughed out of the conversation immediately.

Call to Opportunity

I would like to specify six contemporary areas that are "new opportunities in ministry" for the future, "new-century ministries" already available. But first a caveat. God will still call His servants to traditional pastoral and missions ministries, although those narrow ministries of fifty years ago now represent a smaller portion of the potpourri from which people may choose. Let me develop just a brief paragraph on each of six new opportunities in ministry.

Children. America's schools are inundated with students. All over the country elementary schools are scrambling to find space for over fifty-two million elementary- and secondary-school students, all of whom are candidates for the gospel in churches with a vision to reach out in children's ministry.

Women. The church can no longer consider women second-class citizens or think of them as only wives. They have distinct needs, distinct learning styles, and will require unique ministries for which we are only now beginning to prepare leaders.

Seniors. The maturation of America is here. People aged sixty-five and over now represent a more active, more affluent, more alert group than existed in previous generations. The first "baby boomers" turned fifty in January 1996, and demographers expect as many as one million "boomers" to reach the age of one hundred. Americans over the age of sixty-five have increased their ranks by 50 percent since 1950 and will increase another 75 percent by 2030. They are a special-need group too. I predict that geragogy (the art and science of how older adults learn) will be a popular academic discipline of the future and that churches will be forced to add staff members capable of directing senior adults in ministry as well as ministering to them.

Intercultural/North America. Leaders with focused faith understand that intercultural ministry no longer requires airplanes and furloughs. The Canadian province of British Columbia includes many immigrants from a number of foreign lands. I lived eight years in the triethnic culture of Miami, Florida. In Los Angeles I have taught classes in which 75 percent of the students were Korean. In the Dallas/Fort Worth area minority groups of African Americans, Hispanic Americans, and Asian Americans taken together make up the majority population in Dallas County. If Jesus spoke to His disciples in that city today, He might very well say, "Lift up your eyes and look across the street—the fields are ripe for harvest."

Intercultural/international. Yes, there are still tribes who don't have the Scriptures in their languages, and that's why we still need mission linguists. Yes, there is still a significant place for long-term career missionaries despite the difficulties of raising support, moving a family, and living in another country for most of one's life. Yes, God will call people to do that, but this continent hosts thousands of international students, many of whom will become believers and will return as missionaries to their own countries, capable of serving in their cultures far beyond the capacity of even the brightest migrational missionary. They may very well be the missionaries of the twenty-first century, along with thousands from third-world countries like Korea, which is already sending missionaries around the globe.

Marketplace. Corporate America has discovered a new idea—chaplains. Evangelicals now have the opportunity to take the gospel where we assumed it could go only by casual comment of employees—right into the heart of the pagan American workplace. Our culture is so corrupt, our society so barbaric, that secular companies now grasp the sheer business sense of having a "spiritual leader" on board. What kind of focused faith does one need to take the power of Jesus Christ and the Word of God right into the teeth of the most difficult and corrupt behavior in America, the broader corporate world and daily marketplace?

These are unusual and new opportunities in ministry. Of course, if God has called you to be the pastor of a congregation of 150 on the plains of Iowa, don't go anywhere else. But if the Spirit leads you to become a prison chaplain, a children's pastor, or a church planter, keep your heart open to these new options.

Call to a Specific Place

During my service in Bible colleges and seminaries, I had many discussions with students about ministry options that are "close to relatives," "close to where I went to college," "in the Sunbelt—definitely not Chicago," or "someplace where I could have immediate support from the people I serve." We all have our preferences, and God does not mind our telling Him what we would like; *but the bottom line is what He wants and where He sends.* Here are some reminders:

There are no insignificant places. Every Christian leader must determine his or her ministry gifts and where and how He wants them used. Whether that compares "favorably or unfavorably" with where He sends others has nothing to do with our response to His call. Once in a while colleges and seminaries introduce a chapel speaker as the pastor of a "significant church," and I cringe. Despite our modern passion for evaluating everything by size, I do believe there are no insignificant places if they are places to which God has called us.

There are no small places. Is it more important to be the pastor of a megachurch of five thousand or ten thousand people than the pastor of a community church of seventy-five members? No. Not if God has called you to the latter place. Early in Acts we read about large numbers of people coming to the Lord. But that fades out dramatically even in that transitional book, and no one can tell us how many congregants attended the churches named in the New Testament. There are many small places, but no place is too small to serve God.

There are no impossible places. No doubt there is good reason for leaving a place of ministry on occasion (though too many evangelicals are better "leavers" than "stayers"). But if we are confident of God's call, dependent on His power through the Holy Spirit, and faithful to His Word, the earthly impossible becomes the heavenly possible.

How do we model all this? By showing those we lead how much we value them and how precious we consider God's call to serve them. Our focused faith may refocus *their* faith.

DETERMINED DISCIPLING

What Robert Frost once said about students may be even more accurate when applied to church leaders: "Education is hanging around until you've caught on." In teaching the concept of job control, I have frequently stated in classes and seminars that any kind of job control at the administrative level takes a minimum of one year. When we look at positions in the upper levels of church leadership, one year is hardly long enough to "hang around" if one really intends to produce and reproduce in the New Testament sense of discipleship.

The word *disciple(s)* is not used exclusively for the twelve original followers of Jesus. It appears almost three hundred times in the Gospels and Acts and is used most often to include Christians other than the original Twelve. When Luke referred in Acts to believers, he used the word *saints* three times, *Christians* twice, but *disciples* thirty times. Every true Christian is a learner; therefore every Christian is a disciple.

However, today we use the word *disciple* to refer to a relatively new believer who is being influenced by a leader toward a deeper commitment to Jesus Christ, marked by obedience and a uniquely Christian lifestyle.

Discipling through Cooperation

If a leader does not relate properly to the board, he or she will not have the opportunity to "hang around." And whatever time such leaders serve will be characterized by frustration and tears rather than a mutuality of ministry that leads to reaching goals.

When he returned to Antioch from his first missionary journey, Paul had already attained a stature among first-century Christians that made him a leader to be reckoned with in any decision. His ability in public debate surely could have cowed some of the less-educated disciples and other leaders in the church at Jerusalem. Yet they were in reality the "governing board" of the mother church to whom he was responsible. He was their servant; he understood that relationship, and he behaved in accordance with it.

In any church or ministry organization, board members should set a model for the leadership behavior they want to see in their "employees." But many ministry leaders have advanced beyond some board members in educational, spiritual, social, emotional, and intellectual maturity. The employer-employee relationship calls for deep commitment. As Jesus said, "From everyone who has been given much, much will be demanded; and from the one who has been entrusted with much, much more will be asked" (Luke 12:48).

Discipling through Camaraderie

We could ask who was discipling whom in the Barnabas-Saul relationship at Antioch. Obviously both edified the believers, similar to the way pastors join hands with lay leaders to provide nurture in congregations. I suspect that if you walked into the Antioch church during those years, you would have had a great deal of difficulty ascertaining who was "in charge," so great was the camaraderie among the coworkers.

Leaders must constantly be on guard against jealousies that can immediately destroy the discipling process. Though it may be difficult for a pastor to count other staff members his friends or a college president to maintain similar relationships with his faculty, it is not impossible. Without compromising the dignity of a leadership office, we can develop relationships in which we can say to the members of a multiple staff just what Jesus said to His own disciples: "I no longer call you servants, because a servant does not know his master's business. Instead, I have called you friends, for everything that I learned from my Father I have made known to you" (John 15:15).

Discipling through Community

In seeking to describe a leader's relationship to his staff, it is somewhat difficult to draw an accurate analogy from the ministry of Paul. However, we can look at Aquila and Priscilla, for they were part of the total team ministry, part of the community of believers who served together. They were people whom Paul called "my fellow workers in Christ Jesus" (Rom. 16:3). A sense of community develops when leaders focus on people—that is the point at which discipling must begin (Phil. 2:1–5).

Discipling through Communication

We all share the task of communicating Christian values and a distinctly biblical world-view to our congregations and constituents. Like Paul in Athens, we must speak with clarity and an alertness to contemporary issues, demonstrating our willingness and ability to blaze a trail through the moral mishmash of contemporary pagan society.

We must develop a perspective on contemporary social issues that rests solidly on Scripture, so that we can lead our churches to be the Christian consciences of their communities.

John Throop claims, "In the future, churches, like every other employer, will need to become more skilled at motivating and developing employees. First, however, they should develop a flexible policy and clear, inspiring goals that arise from a compelling vision."[1] Then they must encourage leaders to develop other leaders all along the way by setting ministry standards.

CHAPTER 5
Getting Ready for the Game: Effective Followership

L EONARD BERNSTEIN was once asked, "In an orchestra, which instrument is the most difficult to play?" He immediately responded, "Second fiddle." And so it is in ministry. We buy and read books on leadership and ministry because we see ourselves as leaders. But almost every leader is also a follower, because all of us, like the centurion in the Gospels, serve under authority. In that posture Barnabas served brilliantly as a missionary leader, even after he had apparently been replaced as head of the team. And in the Old Testament we have the wonderful story of Daniel, always a leader, yet always serving under authority.

BIBLICAL BACKGROUND: DANIEL

Perhaps no leadership lessons are more important than those we learn from the quiet consistency of Daniel's relationship with God. What Daniel did in public was possible because of what he had accomplished in private. He maintained a pipeline to heaven, and thus sustained his leadership role by drawing on divine resources.

Maximizing Divine Resources

In Daniel 1:17 we learn that God gave four young men great ability to acquire knowledge and wisdom. They demonstrated an intellectual skill exceptional even among the Chaldeans, who were known as scholars in that day. In addition, Daniel had an unusual ability to understand and interpret the meanings of dreams and visions. God had called him to a special kind of leadership and had equipped him with the resources necessary to implement that leadership.

Certainly people hold positions of leadership to which they have not been called, a posture often producing failure and frustration. Management experts often refer to this phenomenon as "the Peter principle"— bureaucratic organizations often promote people to the level of their incompetence. For example, an adequate youth director becomes a mediocre assistant pastor and later, perhaps, an ineffective senior pastor. Daniel could have been a prime candidate for incompetence in a task that required so much of him. But God gave him resources for the task, and Daniel knew how to maximize those resources.

Maintaining Sincere Humility

Although merely a parenthetical statement in his report to King Nebuchadnezzar, these words of Daniel are significant: "As for me, this mystery has been revealed to me, not because I have greater wisdom than other living men, but so that you, O king, may know the interpretation and that you may understand what went through your mind" (Dan. 2:30).

Both Daniel and Nebuchadnezzar, the righteous servant and the pagan monarch, were minor actors in God's universal theater. He used Nebuchadnezzar to form history, but He used Daniel to form Nebuchadnezzar. No one who carefully reads the Book of Daniel can doubt the doctrine of God's sovereignty.

How easy it is for leaders to take credit when things go well! Daniel knew he had the answer to Nebuchadnezzar's dream; he could have advanced himself significantly by grabbing whatever praise and honor were forthcoming. But in doing so he would have lost favor with God. That Nebuchadnezzar elevated him anyhow is hardly to the point; Daniel could not have known in advance what the results of honest humility would be. Someone once aptly said that there is no limit to the good we can do if we do not care who gets the credit.

Exercising Patience with Peers

You think you have problems with your board? Check out the problems Daniel had as he faced a conspiracy of the presidents and governors in Daniel 6. The penalty for prayer had been announced, and yet, knowing of the king's decree, Daniel continued to pray three times a day. "He got down on his knees and prayed, giving thanks to his God, just as he had done before. Then these men went as a group and found Daniel praying and asking God for help" (Dan. 6:10–11).

Wouldn't it have been easier for Daniel to head right for the throne room of the king and demand that his tormentors be punished? Shouldn't he have designed a confrontational meeting in which they could all share how they felt about the mutual problems of leading the kingdom? But in a time when his peers turned on him and condemned him to his boss, Daniel turned to God.

Daniel's hearty conviction as a youth had not dimmed in his senior years. As an old man Daniel had known political intrigue in one of the greatest pagan capitals the world had ever seen. He had served in the administrations of three monarchs and was still highly esteemed for his skill and integrity. He did not ostentatiously display his spiritual life or deliberately flaunt a religion he considered superior to that of the Babylonians. He prayed neither in the marketplace nor in the palace, but rather in the privacy of his own room. Only by invading his privacy could his enemies find fault with his behavior.

Few models of leadership in the Bible seem more fruitful for our study than Daniel. The responsibility which he held, the blessings God poured on him, and the practical demonstration of his life make the Book of Daniel a focal point of Scripture for all leaders. Let's not forget the central motive of everything Daniel did—faithfulness toward God and consistency toward others. Daniel could be counted on. He was dependable, responsible, and full of genuine integrity, a model servant under authority. God sustained his leadership in alien surroundings because he prepared his heart, served other servants, and handled hurtful criticism in godly fashion.

EXAMINING OUR MOTIVES

During the summer after my sophomore year in college, I traveled to Europe with a ministry team. This was a life-changing experience that reoriented my future. However, summer ministry provided no income for the following fall, so I found myself working throughout my junior year at the RCA television tube manufacturing plant in Marion, Indiana. On my shift, which dragged from 11:00 P.M. to 7:00 A.M, I carried thirty-five-pound television tubes from conveyor belts to a rack and back again. That dreadfully boring and fatiguing work drove me many mornings to remind myself, "I'm doing this now so I don't have to do it the rest of my life."

The job got me through the year and I learned a great deal about perseverance, but my motivation fell far short of the biblical pattern God set for His people in Colossians 3:23: "Whatever you do, work at it with all your heart, as working for the Lord, not for men." Amazingly, this verse appears in the midst of a passage written to slaves, of which there were more than sixty million in the Roman Empire in Paul's day.

As we consider serving under authority, we might review three perspectives of service, three different heart attitudes. These attitudes apply equally to blue-collar jobs on automotive assembly lines in Detroit or to deacons in a church. They describe the way leaders should think about serving under authority and how those attitudes line up with the biblical motivation Paul wrote about in Colossians 3.

Serving Myself

Buffet meals are popular in America because they suit the independent mentality. People think, "Never mind the waitress and all that dining formalism, I'll just go down the line and take what I want. I'll serve myself." That's fine for culinary activities, but in Christian leadership such an attitude reflects our materialistic society.

Unfortunately we often find it in religious roles. Acts 8 tells of Simon Magus and Acts 13 of Elymas the sorcerer, both deeply religious, even claiming association with the God of the Old Testament. In both cases, however, they served themselves, and their fates (as identified by Peter and Paul, respectively) jump at us from the pages of the Bible. Elymas was known as Bar-Jesus ("son of Jesus"), but Paul identified him for what he was—a son of the devil. Even today Christians have a tendency to become like our culture, to get sucked into the selfishness and egoism of the postmodern North American world.

Too often we hear this attitude from those who know better. Pastors and Sunday-school superintendents talk about church size, personal prestige, and even political clout, as though these were somehow spiritual measures of success. They are not. Instead, they reflect the very secular humanism such self-centered leaders claim to be fighting.

Faulty heart preparation corrupts the purity of our service. The old nature postures itself at the center, requiring that all else revolve around it. Humility and meekness, so often demanded in the Scriptures, appear totally absent from any kind of self-serving mentality. Some years ago eight Democratic candidates met for a debate at Dartmouth College. As the audience exited the debate hall, newswriters asked one young coed what she thought of the debate and the candidates. She replied, "None of them seems to have any humility." Her evaluation provides a sad commentary on the attitude of our society and on our political system in which self-serving and self-selling hold constant control.

Such an attitude stands in contrast to Paul's words in Colossians 3:1–4. "Since, then, you have been raised with Christ, set your hearts on things above, where Christ is seated at the right hand of God. Set your minds on things above, not on earthly things. For you died, and your life is now hidden with Christ in God. When Christ, who is your life, appears, then you also will appear with him in glory."

Serving the Organization

As Paul wrote to slaves, he urged them, "Obey your earthly masters in everything; and do it, not only when their eye is on you and to win their favor, but with sincerity of heart and reverence for the Lord" (Col. 3:22). Applying this to our culture today, the word "slaves" could be rendered "employees," giving us a clear mandate. Sacrificial service for a boss, an organization, a school, a church, or a mission board is the proper biblical response in our earthly responsibilities. Many Christian leaders function at this level and serve admirably under authority.

King William II of Prussia found himself in trouble. With no money left in the imperial treasury for wars and rebuilding, the king asked the women of the land to bring their gold and silver jewelry to be melted down. In return they received a decoration of iron stamped "I gave gold for iron, 1813." Surprisingly these symbols became prized more than the jewelry, for they offered proof that the women had sacrificed for their king. Indeed, jewelry became unfashionable and the Order of the Iron Cross was born.

The Christian works hard not just while the boss watches and not just for recognition. Our society loses over $100 billion a year to various kinds of cheating—pilferage in department stores, office supplies taken home by employees, improper usage of postage meters, default on student loans, and other kinds of "white-collar crime." According to the New Testament, leaders must resist this kind of attitude and serve ministry organizations with integrity.

Remember, too, the biblical message to bosses: "Masters, provide your slaves what is right and fair, because you know that you also have a Master in heaven" (4:1). This verse addresses supervisors of every kind—managers, foremen, pastors, principals, missionary executives. All Christians share this common responsibility to model integrity and honesty. Then service for the organization becomes a spiritual duty and even a daily joy. But there remains a better way.

Serving the Lord

The heart of this passage aims at our hearts, pointing up the motive of our service as *committed Christians.* "Whatever you do, work at it with all your heart, as working for the Lord, not for men, since you know that you will receive an inheritance from the Lord as a reward. It is the Lord Christ you are serving. Anyone who does wrong will be repaid for his wrong, and there is no favoritism" (Col. 3:23–25).

The clear imperative of this passage implores believers to "work at it with all your hearts." Only here in the New Testament do we find the phrase "working for the Lord," and the context offers a distinctively biblical heart preparation. How can you and I actually make this work in ministry leadership? The text seems to require at least three assurances.

1. Assurance that God has called us to do what we do. Does God really want me pastoring children rather than working in a laboratory? Am I really to be a missionary rather than a computer programmer? Am I following through in God's will for my life?
2. Assurance of meeting needs. Few of us can sustain energy and enthusiasm for some ministries over a long period of time unless we have motivation other than a paycheck. Industrial psychologists tell us there must be self-actualization, and the best kind comes with the knowledge that we're meeting the needs of other people.
3. Assurance of God's blessing. If God can use me to further His work, to share the gospel with others, to be an encouragement to my peers, or in some other significant way, then I know I am genuinely serving Christ.

Paul reminded the Colossians that they would receive an inheritance from the Lord (3:24). But he added a negative feature, "anyone who does wrong will be repaid for his wrong" (3:25).

Colossians 3:1–17 deals with the personal spiritual life, and verses 18–21 discuss relationships. Only when these two dimensions of life are in order can we properly turn our attention to serving Christ in public ministry. Success "on the job" can be properly interpreted only in the light of these larger priorities. To put it another way, no service is acceptable to God if it perverts His priorities of personal spiritual life and solid family unity.

Elizabeth Elliot tells a marvelous story, which I paraphrase here. It takes the form of a fable in which the disciples were one day asked by the Lord to carry stones throughout the day. Each chose the smallest stone he could find; then in the evening the Lord turned their stones into bread. With hungry stomachs they went to bed, wishing they had chosen larger stones.

The next day He gave the same command. Imagine how the disciples scurried around picking the largest stones they could carry. As they made camp for the night, Peter, expecting to feast on fresh bread, asked, "Lord, what should we do with our stones?" "Oh," said the Lord, "just roll them into the river." The complaining sounded like the Israelites of old and was only quelled when the Lord asked, "For whom did you carry your stones today?"

Some leaders serve themselves; others serve the organization—church, school, or mission board; but those who really understand the motivational principles of the New Testament serve the Lord.

SERVING OTHER SERVANTS

About two hundred years ago there lived in Dublin, Ireland, a brilliant theologian and writer named Jonathan Swift, dean of Saint Patrick's Cathedral. He is perhaps most commonly remembered for his classic tale, *Gulliver's Travels*, originally written as a satire on "little men" holding high public office.

We know the book as a children's classic describing the adventures of Captain Lemuel Gulliver, captain and surgeon, and the only survivor of the wreck of the good ship *Antelope*. His discovery of the Isle of Lilliput with its six-inch inhabitants called Lilliputians is one of the great fictional tales of all times.

Swift was right. There are "small" people. Perhaps not on an Isle of Lilliput but certainly not only in the world of fantasy. They exist in the real world, and we see their smallness in their character, not their stature. All of us have known political, moral, and social Lilliputians. What concerns us most in the church, however, are spiritual Lilliputians. Yet a major portion of our task, especially in the middle-management arena, is to serve people both up and down the ministry ladder. And rather than pushing the ladder away, we want to help them climb.

Equipping God's Servants

In Ephesians 4:12 Paul wrote about the need to equip believers to serve the Lord. The word "prepare" (NIV) renders the Greek verb *katartizō*, which is also translated "equipping" (NASB, NKJV) or "perfecting" (KJV). Perhaps a better rendering is "repairing." When Jesus found the first disciples, they were repairing (*katartizō*) their nets by the Sea of Galilee (Matt. 4:21). Paul used that same word in this passage to talk about equipping saints for ministry.

Some believers are "broken," others are incomplete. Some are tired because of long service and hard work. Effective Christian leadership helps put them into working order so their tasks of ministry can continue.

Proper leadership facilitates the work of others, making it possible for them to carry out their tasks. Leaders who are interested in "repairing" or equipping others value the differences in people and offer nonjudgmental approaches to their problems. Biblical leaders are to be faithful servants serving servants.

Enriching God's Servants

We hear much these days about "enrichment" programs in education. The term generally refers to something a bit extra, a little beyond the minimal requirements. Leaders who enrich others help them accept themselves; and feeling wanted is essential to self-acceptance. Sometimes a search for security in a marriage partner, friends, or relatives may reflect a person's need for self-confidence. People who dislike themselves rarely love others, and so they become candidates for depression and self-centeredness. This is seen in the life of King Saul (1 Sam. 9:20–21; 10:20–22). Enriching the lives of our colleagues by assuring them that we love and support them enables them to grow as people, as Christians, and as leaders.

Encouraging God's Servants

Management research shows that informing workers that their work is significant gives them powerful motivation for doing their best. We all try harder when someone needs us!

A study of a petroleum company uncovered the fact that many of their gas-station attendants had feelings of inferiority, resulting in careless attitudes and low productivity. So the company reminded them that they were often responsible for their customers' lives, so they should inspect their cars properly. The workers came to understand that promptness and efficient service were important to their customers. Awareness of job importance led to a higher quality of performance.

People need to be what God has made them, rather than playing unfamiliar roles superimposed on them by church leaders. We encourage by emphasizing their strengths. Andrew Carnegie said, "Take away my people but leave my factories and soon grass will grow on the factory floors. Take away my factories but leave my people and soon we will have new and better factories."[1] In any Christian organization—church, mission board, college, or publishing house—every person holds tremendous importance. By encouragement we can reduce the number of unproductive people who do not grasp this sense of significance and responsibility.

HANDLING HURTFUL CRITICISM

It happens to all of us. And the higher the leadership post, the more common the experience of serving the Lord under fire. Every church has fair-weather workers, soldiers willing to do battle so long as things go well. We all desperately need more soldiers who know how to serve under fire, people who can stay at their posts even when the rockets of criticism explode all around them.

David learned early in his adult life how criticism can be a bitter pill. The Philistines, with whom he had been living while on the run from Saul, had gathered at Aphek to battle the Israelites, and David planned to make the trip with them. But King Achish dismissed David, probably suspecting his real loyalty to Israel, and sent him and his men back to Ziklag, their headquarters in exile.

When David and his men returned to Ziklag, they saw that the Amalekites had attacked Ziklag and burned it, and all their women and children had been kidnapped (1 Sam. 30:1–3). The situation was so desperate that it brought David and his men to tears "until they had no strength left to weep" (30:4).

Then an amazing thing happened. Rather than making plans immediately for liberating their wives and children, the faithful few who had followed David in his flight from Saul turned on *him* and even spoke of stoning him, so great was their grief over the disaster at Ziklag (30:6).

Imagine David's predicament! His wives and children had been taken captive too; the Philistines had refused his help after he had graciously offered it; and now his few loyal friends talked of killing him as though the attack on Ziklag had been entirely his fault!

No doubt David learned some important lessons that day about taking criticism, lessons that came back to his mind many times during his long years as a king. Criticism can bring new insights about ourselves, our ministries, and the world around us. But it can be a bitter "low blow" when given at an inopportune time from an unexpected source.

Types of Criticism

Constructive criticism is best offered orally. Implied criticism may more easily be misunderstood, even when its intentions are noble. It often takes the form of a sarcastic comment and can quickly fester into open conflict, leading to the disruption of friendships and perhaps even a church split. If you find it necessary to criticize someone with the objective of building up that person in a positive sense, do it face to face with good manners and honesty in an atmosphere of spiritual dignity.

Criticism should never be destructive, implied, or unfair. Wise leaders show great concern for the feelings of others (Phil. 2:14) and add a solid dose of kindness to judgment. Wise criticism gives the criticized person an opportunity to make personal adjustments and the time to correct mistakes.

Sources of Criticism

Criticism can come to us (or at us) from superiors, peers, subordinates, the general public, friends, and even from ourselves. Perhaps the best way to analyze these is to use one example, a Sunday school teacher in a local church.

Criticism from a *superior* might be a word from a departmental superintendent that this teacher has arrived consistently late for Sunday school. That would be a necessary and positive piece of criticism if fair, spoken, and constructive.

The same teacher could also receive criticism from another teacher at the *peer* level. If spoken in love and with genuine concern, that friend exercises a Christian duty to offer constructive comment about some aspect of her sister's ministry.

Criticism from a *subordinate*, perhaps a student, is more difficult to handle. Often it doesn't come person-to-person because others fear speaking with us about the matter. So criticism often takes the form of complaining to others until little cliques form, some of which think the critic is right and the leader unfair, while others, taking the side of the leader, rush to tell her what is being said about her.

Criticism from *the general public* is to be expected. There will always be people who do not understand or agree with what we do or why we do it. In the teacher illustration, such criticism might come from the parents of one of the students or perhaps a member of the church who does not support the Sunday-school program and seizes every opportunity to say so.

Criticism from a *friend* is most difficult to take, as David discovered. Nevertheless it becomes valuable if we trust the person who offers it.

Self-criticism ought to be going on continually. But let's not push this so far that we become compulsive, demanding more of ourselves than we can deliver. An overdose of self-criticism can diminish self-worth and create feelings of inferiority that become destructive to ministry.

Responding to Criticism

Perhaps the first guideline in handling criticism is to *consider the source*. Criticism from a supervisor or a friend certainly would be more valuable than criticism from the general public. But even "enemies" can help us if we're willing to extract value from their words.

Always remember to *maintain your security*. Our natural reaction when criticized is to fight back and become defensive, offering excuses for the behavior under attack. Such defensiveness almost always leads to emotional reactions rather than rational responses.

Don't counterattack. This irrational response rests on the assumption that the critic's motives are improper and his information inaccurate. Even potentially constructive criticism can quickly degenerate into a fight if we insist on an immediate counterattack.

Try to determine whether the criticism is justifiable. When others point out weaknesses or flaws in our ministry, they serve us well. When we *validate the report* and make the correction, we ought to thank the critic.

Learn what you can from the criticism. We can grow even in the most negative and unfair situations. Perhaps only a greater humility before God and greater dependence on the Holy Spirit can help us handle these moments in our lives. Remember the scriptural key to handling criticism: "A gentle answer turns away wrath, but a harsh word stirs up anger" (Prov. 15:1). This axiom deserves memorization and regular use.

Bob Radcliffe compares the role of associate church staff members with that second-chair violinist we talked about at the beginning of this chapter. "A few of the issues for an associate to consider in a relationship with the senior pastor of a church are assessing integrity, authority and power, communication patterns, and salary and benefits. The more that can be discovered about this crucial relationship before accepting the call, the better. Not all can be discovered before the call, but it is important to know what to look for, so that the associate is not surprised when it is found. The first-chair player has a very important role in the ministry of the associate, and the associate would be very wise to recognize that fact and learn to work with the senior pastor so they can develop into all that God wants them be. Beautiful music comes no other way."[2]

Not all of us under authority serve in an associate pastor role, but Radcliffe's comments can quickly and easily be adapted to any relationship between ourselves and those who supervise our work. The example of Daniel looms large.

CHAPTER 6
Keep Your Eye on the Ball: Goal Achievement

IN THAT REMARKABLY PHILOSOPHICAL FANTASY, *Alice in Wonderland*, Alice comes to the crossroads and asks directions of the Cheshire Cat.

"Which road should I take?" she asks.

"Well, where do you want to go?" the cat asks.

"I don't know," she replies.

The cat responds, "Then it doesn't matter which road you take."

Which is the most significant characteristic of administrative leadership. Credibility? Courage? Critical thinking? In my view *purpose* leads the list—the ability to set and achieve goals. But goal achievement is not a personality trait; it is learned behavior. Patrick Lenciono speaks to this issue in the context of business and industry. "The most important principle that an executive must embrace is a desire to produce results. As obvious as this sounds, it is not universally practiced by the highest-ranking executives in many companies. Many CEOs put something ahead of results on their list of priorities, and it represents the most dangerous of all the temptations: the desire to protect the status of their careers."[1]

Of course, Christ-centered leaders are not interested in pushing results without the crucial ameliorating factors of biblical meekness and servanthood. Yet leaders are expected to get things done, and if they don't they won't be leaders very long. They may carry titles, hold positions, and in some cases, even draw large salaries—*but leadership means helping groups of people achieve goals.*

BIBLICAL BACKGROUND: PRISCILLA AND AQUILA

As businesspeople, Aquila and Priscilla were probably quite accustomed to goal achievement. By the standards of the first-century Mediterranean world they were well skilled, well traveled, and possibly well off. But in a quiet way their collaborative efforts in ministry led to the achievement of many church-planting goals in association with their friend Paul.

Rarely in Scripture do we read about husband-and-wife teams who effectively served Christ as a couple. But Luke always mentioned Aquila and Priscilla together, and of the six times their names appear, Priscilla is named first in four of them. Paul met them when he was in Corinth. "After this, Paul left Athens and went to Corinth. There he met a Jew named Aquila, a native of Pontus, who had recently come from Italy with his wife Priscilla, because Claudius had ordered all the Jews to leave Rome. Paul went to see them, and because he was a tentmaker as they were, he stayed and worked with them" (Acts 18:1–3).

The meeting in Corinth occurred because first-century tentweavers tended to gather in the same part of town. Unlike Barnabas and Luke, Priscilla and Aquila never left their paying ministries to serve Christ. So far as we know, everywhere they went they engaged in their trade, using proceeds to advance the cause of the New Testament church. They teach us some important lessons about leadership:

- For the Christian there is no difference between sacred and secular duty.
- Lay leaders can serve Christ effectively without leaving their jobs.
- Work is a gift from God, not the result of sin.

Priscilla and Aquila stayed in Corinth for about two years (around A.D. 51–52) and then moved on with Paul to Ephesus, where the couple ministered privately to the zealous Apollos. Imagine this sophisticated couple, theologically precise and literate, listening to the bright young Alexandrian Jew as he preached in the Ephesian synagogue. After hearing him preach, they decided that eloquence and fervency of spirit were insufficient for a mature ministry, so they coached him further in the Scriptures (18:18–26).

From Ephesus they went back to Rome and were serving there when Paul wrote his epistle to believers in that city: "Greet Priscilla and Aquila, my fellow workers in Christ Jesus. They risked their lives for me. Not only I but all the churches of the Gentiles are grateful to them. Greet also the church that meets at their house" (Rom. 16:3–5).

Several years later Priscilla and Aquila apparently returned to Ephesus (based on 2 Tim. 4:19, in which Paul asked Timothy, who was in Ephesus, to greet Priscilla and Aquila for him). However, their behavior, not their mobility, serves as our focus. Once again, several important lessons grab our attention.

- People who achieve ministry goals prioritize the local church. Wherever Priscilla and Aquila went they were active not only in ministry but also in a local congregation, which met in their home in Rome (Rom. 16:5).
- Hospitality is an important Christian virtue. Using one's resources— time, money, space, wisdom, learning, skills—lies at the heart of achieving ministry goals.

Of interest is the fact that they encouraged Paul, their friend and coworker, in three major cities over a period of about sixteen years.[2] This husband-and-wife team ministered as "laypersons" together. Family models are essential in ministry organizations, and we can rejoice to have this record of a loving couple, whose song of service for Christ seems to have been sung as a duet.

UNDERSTANDING GOAL ACHIEVEMENT

Humorist Robert Benchley once suggested that the world could be divided into two groups—those who divide the world into two groups and those who don't. Perhaps. But surely churches and other Christian ministries can be divided into two groups—those who have focused their direction for the twenty-first century and those who have not. Clear objectives take aim at the future with the real world in clear perspective. In tennis we have an important step called "racquet preparation." As the ball comes toward you, it is important to pull the racquet back in preparation for the next shot. This chapter centers on ministry preparation.

Herb Miller, president of Net Results, considers purposeful behavior one of the "twelve oft-overlooked qualities of spirit that determine [a person's] effectiveness as a leader." He says, "People who risk making changes not only succeed more often, they also fail more often. Effective leaders are so completely committed to their vision and projects, however, that they see setbacks as opportunities rather than dead ends. . . . When they fail, they forgive themselves and move on. When they fall down, they pick themselves up, figure out why they fell, and try again (with the added advantage of having learned from a mistake)."[3]

How do we grasp goal-achieving behavior which makes possible such a concentration on results? How do we go about what God wants from us in such a way that we hit what we aim for most of the time? How do we meet the expectations of the leadership team and the wider group while performing at a level of excellence? In other words, how do we keep focused on our goals? Clearly the essential first step in achieving goals is setting them, the very point at which many leaders fail.

Personal Life

Can you identify your life goals? Have you ever written them down? Meaningless expenditure of time tends toward purposelessness and kills motivation. In our "pressure-cooker" age we do well to remember David's words in Psalm 31:15, "My times are in your hands." If God sovereignly controls time, then insufficient time—a common complaint among leaders—is neither the problem nor an excuse for things left undone. *The weakness lies in our not planning and not investing our time wisely.*

Many of us find ourselves in a position of constant *reaction*. Rather than controlling the events of a given day as much as possible, we tend to be governed constantly by the events themselves. Rather than managing our time, we allow our time to manage us. We exercise our leadership like a small boy with a large dog on a leash. Wherever the dog wants to go, he simply tugs the boy along.

The secret of successful leadership is to live and move *above* the circumstances and thereby exercise as much control over them as possible. This does not in any way usurp the authority of God as sovereign Controller of all circumstances; instead it encourages us to discover His will and then to seek to fulfill that will by a constant pattern of goal achievement.

When I was facing a job change at age thirty-five, I decided to write out my lifetime purposes. That document, which I found useful for the next three decades, reads as follows:

> In accord with the will of God and my understanding of Scripture, I want to be moving toward attainment in dimensions of a well-rounded life as described in the following purposes: *Spiritually*, to be a growing Christian who matures consistently in learning and serving; *physically*, to keep my body in good health and strong physical condition; *intellectually*, to use and expand mental resources in both knowledge and wisdom; *socially*, to recognize and fulfill my responsibility to family, church, government, and other social groups; *professionally*, to exercise positive and progressive leadership in Christian higher education and, more specifically, theological education at graduate and undergraduate levels; and *culturally*, to recognize that all beauty and truth ultimately comes from God and therefore to seek to broaden the cultural and aesthetic tastes of myself, my family, and my students.

As a leader, you should have some kind of life statement that keeps you on target, though yours, of course, may differ from mine.

Present Ministry

"Ministry by objectives" is the process of managing a Christian organization based on identifying its mission and establishing a realistic program for achieving its goals and objectives.

What specific behaviors can help focus your ministry?
- Define the mission
- Assess strengths and weaknesses
- Prepare measurable objectives
- Develop strategies to use available resources
- Practice accountability with the leadership team
- Design short-range and long-range plans
- Revise processes and strategies as necessary
- Evaluate progress all along the way

In discussing what they call "new skills for new leadership roles," Caela Farren and Beverly Kaye identify what they call "the most indispensable of all the leadership roles. Leaders are bridges that connect people to the future. They include others' visions in their own, building alliances and partnerships based on shared aspirations. Taking the long view will make us more effective leaders today and will carry us through our uncertain times to the future we dared to create."[4]

Public Service

In reality all ministry is public service, but I want to distinguish here between what we do in our "assigned" responsibilities and the wider view of serving the Lord. Most pastors and Christian leaders serve the Lord in places in addition to their churches or organizations. So their focus should expand to include involvement in what is called "project organization." Generally such projects would not extend beyond a year in duration, though there may be some notable exceptions, such as a centennial celebration that requires working on the project for two or three years before the event.

For the sake of illustration, assume that you are the chairperson of the annual community prayer breakfast responsible for planning that event. The breakfast requires achieving your objectives through certain steps.

- Develop the general "characteristics" of the project and establishing overall objectives.
- Prepare the specifics, including date, time, place, and financing.
- Establish what is called "supportability" for the plans already made. In other words, can the committee actually carry out the requirements which you have set for the project?
- Determine the equipment and other resources needed. Will this breakfast be held at a public restaurant? What kinds of facilities will you need for the event?
- Publicize the event.
- Develop a plan that will enable you to meet your objectives. Should there be preparation on the part of your staff before they go to the breakfast site? How will you coordinate training sessions with their already busy schedules?

- Evaluate the event. After the breakfast has been held, your team should analyze the results. How many attended? What feedback have you heard? How could this event be improved next time?

Once you have written specific and measurable objectives for key ministry areas, you should seek to gain consensus on those objectives from everyone involved. Then develop strategies on how to use available resources to meet objectives. The following is an example from higher education.

Until accrediting associations shake them loose and encourage them to restructure their thinking, colleges (like most churches) tend to put budget planning before educational planning. Financial officers and budget committees tell academic leaders the boundaries of the budget and expect them to supervise the learning process within those boundaries. This wrongheaded approach to resource allocation convolutes the whole process. *In colleges and seminaries, academic planning must precede budget planning. In churches and missions, ministry planning must precede budget planning. If we fail on this point, we will quickly become budget-driven rather than mission-driven, and the wrong group of sailors will control the rudder.*

The goals and objectives of a ministry organization must deal with every aspect of the ministry, not just those that are popular, clamor for attention, or frequently face fiscal disaster. Being goal achievers means we proceed from our mission to our overall objectives, to specific goals, to definable action steps or strategies. Though an organization's mission need be revisited only once every several years, we must be ready to change or modify objectives, goals, or strategies.

CONTROLLING YOUR PRIORITIES

Consider the impact of Jesus' familiar words in Matthew 9:38: "Ask the Lord of the harvest, therefore, to send out workers into his harvest field." Unfortunately we seldom associate verses 35–36, which describe a human harvest, with verse 38. "Jesus went through all the towns and villages, teaching in their synagogues, preaching the good news of the kingdom and healing every disease and sickness. When he saw the crowds, he had compassion on them, because they were harassed and helpless, like sheep without a shepherd." The words "harassed and helpless" certainly are an apt description of many people today.

As we understand the mission of almost any church or ministry organization, we realize we must minister to people as they are in today's world, people who are harassed (the Greek word rendered "harassed" means "to be distressed, troubled," and the Greek word "helpless" means "to be cast down, lying prostrate"). It does no good to evoke images of D. L. Moody and Charles Spurgeon preaching two-hour sermons or George Whitefield gathering thousands in the fields. Our ministries must serve *today's* people—people whose world is dominated by mobility, media, and materialism. We have educated a generation of watchers who are well-versed in electronic machinery but often are ignorant in relationships. In such a climate we must be sure our priorities are correct. In this connection think about the following four questions.

What Is Essential?

Christian leaders cannot let circumstances and their surrounding struggles determine what is really important. Achieving goals in any church organization means we need to decide what is most important and also to identify what is unimportant. When an emergency-room physician quickly assesses the status of an accident victim, he or she may realize immediately that a crushed forearm will need major surgery, but stopping the bleeding is the immediate priority.

Leaders organize their lives so priorities come first, even if some other things may not get done. With many people asking us to do many things, we need to understand the essentials.

- What is the mission of your ministry? How has it changed from what it was, and how might it change in the future?
- In what ways have you translated the mission into specific targets and assignments (that is, goals and objectives)?
- What strategies can you use to concentrate your resources toward meeting your goals?
- Have all phases of your ministry been included in goal-setting and planning?

When Must It Be Done?

Urgency so closely relates to importance that we sometimes assume they go together. But they don't. Some things are absolute essentials but are not necessarily urgent. Others (like stopping the bleeding of an injured person) demonstrate immediate connection between the essential and the urgent. It may be necessary to counsel a deacon regarding a public outburst of anger at the last business meeting, but that need not be done immediately. On the other hand, if an annual board meeting takes place tomorrow, it would be appropriate to take some time today to review the agenda and make sure your support documents are in order.

Who Will Do It?

Since not everything is of equal importance, and not everything must be done now or even soon, how can team leaders effectively delegate to others what they should *not* do? *Remember that decision-making, like power, naturally moves upward in an organization.* Like hot air, if we want it closer to the action on the floor, we have to force it down in some way. That's why mature ministry coaches don't make any decision that can be made by someone closer to the line of action and don't take on tasks that should be done by someone else.

Micromanagers may be successful in achieving goals, but they rarely develop leadership in people around them. If your priorities are shaky and your goals end up in the drawer instead of the win column, you might ask yourself how well you relate to other stakeholders and players. Richard Hackman suggests that we ask ourselves four questions in this connection:

- *Who decides?* Who has the right to make decisions about how the work will be carried out and to determine how problems that develop will be resolved?
- *Who is responsible?* Where do responsibility and accountability for performance outcomes ultimately reside?
- *Who gains?* How are monetary rewards allocated among the individuals and groups that help generate them?
- *Who learns?* How are opportunities, growth, and career advancement distributed among organization members?[5]

How Will We Know It Is Achieved?

Each question in this section leads to the next: Importance raises the question of urgency, urgency raises the question of responsibility, and responsibility raises the question of evaluation. We know goals are achieved when we build in ways to evaluate. For a classroom teacher that might be a test at the end of a study unit. For a college, it might be an alumni survey. For an employer, an exit interview would help. The danger here is to make ministry measurement *quantitative*, whereas the New Testament focuses on *quality*. Since evaluation depends on goals, the more shaky and shabby your goals, the less likely you will be able to do effective evaluation.

Suppose a church hires a new youth director. They give him a simple one-page job description, and at the end of the year he comes up for evaluation by the church board. On what basis will they evaluate his ministry? Did he follow the pastor's orders? Did the young people like him? Are the parents satisfied? Has the youth group grown numerically? As important and obvious as all of those factors are, we must check "none of the above."

A senior pastor and a church board should evaluate a youth director on the basis of clear-cut objectives they set out at the beginning of the year. If satisfying the parents was written and agreed on, then a few phone calls can solve the evaluation issue. But if personal spiritual growth in the lives of teenagers forms the major objective and priority, the board needs to figure out some way to measure that objective before they decide how well the youth director is functioning. If we haven't identified essential priorities, we can't evaluate achievement levels.

Sometimes achievement can be quantifiable, such as the number of visits a pastor might make in a given month, or expanding the day-care center to five days instead of two. Often, however, we look for life change as an evaluation of achieved ministry goals. A pastor whose congregation seems self-centered and preoccupied with its own programs and buildings may see a long-term goal achieved when those same people learn how to function as an interdependent congregation that shows concern for people. A mission field director who leads people highly skilled in their specialties but ineffective as a ministry team might praise God for

74

helping them develop unity and a genuinely cooperative spirit that produces team results.

James Kouzes and Barry Posner emphasize the necessity of transferring leadership responsibility from the chief executive office and spreading it around the ranks.

From what we observed in our research, as more and more people answer the call, we will rejoice in the outcome. For we discovered, and rediscovered, that leadership is not the private reserve of a few charismatic men and women. It is a process that ordinary people use when they are bringing forth the best from themselves and others. We believe that whether you are in the private sector or the public sector, whether you are an employee or a volunteer, whether you are on the front line or in the senior echelon, whether you are a student or a parent, you are capable of developing yourself as a leader far more than tradition has ever assumed possible. When we liberate the leader in everyone, extraordinary things happen.[6]

CHAPTER 7
Looking Down the Field: Strategic Planning

IN 1999 TALK OF Y2K and the new millennium jammed virtually
every media outlet. Self-proclaimed pioneers and survivalists dug
shelters and stockpiled food. Thousands wondered whether the global monetary system would crash.

If Christ was born in 5 B.C. or 4 B.C., as many New Testament scholars
claim, then that fearful millennial transition to the year 2000 had already
come and gone. But consider the upside—many people were looking to
the future with a new intensity, and for many Christian leaders that provides a refreshing change. Though contemporary management literature
doesn't talk much about planning ("vision casting" is the new jargon), we
can never minimize the necessity for careful planning.

BIBLICAL BACKGROUND: JOSEPH

Young Joseph found himself in Egypt shortly after 1900 B.C. Through a
series of events that surely must have seemed unfortunate to him at the
time, he languished in prison after a promising start as a steward in
Potiphar's household. Even after the chief butler had been restored to his
position in the palace, Joseph waited two more years. Who would have
thought that God, in His infinite wisdom, would design managerial training for Joseph in such a place? Planners need experience, and Joseph gained
valuable years of that commodity in a most unfriendly place. In prison he

held a position of responsibility (Gen. 39:22–23), and there God built into him the qualities of patience, serenity of spirit, and maturity of judgment that he would need in the decades ahead.

The need for a qualified leader to carry out the planning process is no less important today than in ancient Egypt. Whether a five-year plan for a local church or a ten-year plan for a college or seminary, the process calls for men and women who have experience and the gifts of wisdom and administration.

Vital Insight

Joseph's handling of Pharaoh's dream rested, at least in part, on his philosophy of history. He understood that God controlled the past, the present, and the future—even in the land of Egypt. God decided to show Pharaoh what He would do so that Pharaoh would understand the finality of His word.

Planners with vital insight and biblical balance do not see present and future responsibilities compromised by the reality of Christ's return. Working-while-watching is the byword of Jesus' parables. Selling one's property, clothing oneself in a white sheet, and climbing to the top of a nearby mountain to wait for Jesus reflects cultic sectarianism, not evangelical Christianity.

Accurate Information

The only intelligent way to envision the future is to find out as much as possible about the past and the present. That is why it is so much more difficult to handle the planning process in a new ministry than in one that has some background history. Note how Joseph had access to key data: "Then Pharaoh said to Joseph, 'Since God has made all this known to you, there is no one so discerning and wise as you. You shall be in charge of my palace, and all my people are to submit to your orders. Only with respect to the throne will I be greater than you' " (Gen. 41:39–41).

If your supervisor or board expects you to take responsibility for long-range planning, be sure you have the information necessary to project the kind of vision that will carry the ministry on into the future. But there is a second important step here—working to find the information you need. Joseph set an example here, for he "went out from Pharaoh's presence and traveled throughout Egypt" (41:46).

Joseph's responsibilities required footwork to see exactly what he faced. In our situation it is more likely that hard drives, diskettes, or file folders of old minutes will do the job. But the same principle applies: Long-range planning does not operate well in an information vacuum.

Once gathered, the information remains useless until we develop a system for using it. Genesis 47:13–26 reviews the severity of the famine and the process Joseph used to gather first the money, then the land, and eventually the people for Pharaoh.

All this looks like a repressive monarchy which, of course, it was. We may wonder why the Holy Spirit would lead Joseph into such circumstances. But we cannot superimpose our modern cultural standards on the historical setting of Joseph's situation any more than we can read New Testament patterns of leadership back into the Book of Genesis.

Practical Implementation

In the previous chapter we talked about goals and objectives, essential foundations for planning. Joseph mapped out the kind of organization necessary to make his plan work: someone making the basic decisions; overseers directing the storing of one-fifth of the harvest in each of the next seven years; workers gathering food into strategically located storage cities; and others providing distribution as needed. The first ingredient of practical implementation is a specific plan.

But Joseph also built in corrective measures for problem-solving (Gen. 47:1–31). As the plan unfolded, he had sufficient flexibility to handle more and more people coming for more and more help.

The results of Joseph's efforts were at least three: the saving of his family, the saving of the fledging family/nation of Israel, and the saving of Egypt. Let's not think of Joseph as a frightened boy thrown into a pit by his brothers or a strange psychic who could interpret dreams. He was one of the most astute administrative leaders in all history, and the Scriptures offer in some detail the account of his efforts in long-range planning.

UNDERSTANDING THE TASK

Louis A. Allen defines planning as "the work a manager performs to predetermine a course of action."[1] He includes seven basic steps or aspects to the planning process:

- *Forecasting:* the work a manager performs to estimate the future.
- *Establishing objectives:* the work a manager performs to determine the end results to be accomplished.
- *Programming:* the work a manager performs to establish the sequence and priority of action steps to be followed in reaching objectives.
- *Scheduling:* the work a manager performs to establish a time sequence for programmed steps.
- *Budgeting:* the work a manager performs to allocate resources necessary to accomplish objectives.
- *Establishing procedures:* the work a manager performs to develop and apply standardized methods of performing specified work.
- *Developing policies:* the work a manager performs to develop and interpret standing decisions that apply to repetitive questions and problems of significance to the enterprise as a whole.[2]

In its simplest form planning attempts to forecast future developments and then to devise a program in line with those developments or at least to fit into them in order to continue accomplishing the organization's objectives and fulfilling its mission.

Mission and Objectives

Planning helps us identify the winds of change in order to set our sails more effectively. This is not to suggest that the winds themselves determine the direction of the organizational vessel. However, knowing the direction of the wind and the tide, leaders can more correctly steer the vessel to the intended port.

The planning process relates to the target, that is, looking down the field. Assume that you will be the planning leader for a church of approximately 250 members. To make any headway at all in long-range planning, you must delineate objectives to cover all aspects of the church and to describe those ministries as specifically as possible. Being specific about objectives means more than just being committed to worship, fellowship, instruction, service, and evangelism. Each of these five categories of church life raises important issues that we must take into consideration in our planning. In short, organizations with fuzzy objectives will also have inadequate or inaccurate planning.

Measuring Planning Responsibility

How much time does each person in the organization give to planning and how far in advance is that time invested? Planning needs thought, and various leaders in the organization should devote time to thinking about the future. Ideally, senior pastors should give only a small percentage of their planning time to the immediate present, a larger percent to activities a month ahead, and the most time to ministries projected beyond three to five years. The American Management Association suggests that in long-range vision-casting at least a third of the leaders' time be given to planning.

The axiom is clear: The higher the level of leadership in the organization, the greater the responsibility for long-range planning. This also means that individuals in higher levels of leadership need to give less time to immediate concerns.

Management by Objectives

Twenty years ago management by objectives (called MBO) was one of the most popular concepts in administrative procedure. Unfortunately it became an all-purpose term meaning whatever a particular user chose to define by it. MBO helped us look at administration as a whole rather than as a mere series of procedures. The principle is simple: We measure progress only in terms of goal achievement.

Ministry by objectives can mean basically the same thing in the church. A congregation that adequately defines its mission must emphasize goals to be reached and must then design a plan for achievement.

Mission and Vision

I once heard a quotation attributed to Bobby Knight, well-known coach of the University of Indiana basketball team: "The will to succeed is important, but what's more important is the will to prepare." People who plan reflect the will to prepare. They also link two absolutely essential components of effective leadership—mission and vision. Remember—*mission* describes the reason for our existence, what God has called us to do.

Congregations, mission agencies, and parachurch organizations must draw boundaries that *de*fine but do not *con*fine. Mission statements can and should be reduced to a clear and concise sentence, or at the most, to a brief paragraph.

Vision, as we have already noted, describes what we will do in the future to carry out our God-given mission. *Planning forms a bridge between mission and vision, a link without which we cannot make that journey.* Yet the average pastor spends less than two hours a week planning and thinking. According to research, most pastors spend about ten hours a week in sermon preparation, nine hours in "miscellaneous activities," six hours in prayer and personal devotions, with the remaining time spent in a variety of activities such as evangelism, training leaders, and mediating conflict.

However, LaRue says pastors spend *fifteen* hours a week in miscellaneous activities and preparing for or attending meetings. There may be great potential for reorganization in that block of time; portions of it should be given to the leadership roles of planning, thinking, and developing others.[3]

Certainly "envisioning" seems a much more exciting process than "planning," but we cannot avoid their inseparability. Congregations without vision may survive, but they do not move toward ministry potential. Max De Pree wrote this about vision:

> Part of an organization's vision can be an ideal toward which we always strive without ever reaching it. Part of a vision must be attainable, lest the group lose hope. A good idea does not a vision make. Without some risk attached, a good idea remains nothing more. With some risk, with some promise of change, with a touch of the unattainable, a good idea may just become the vision for a group. Visions are liable to fail. A vision can never be guaranteed, no matter what the price or source.

A group's vision can come from one person or many people, but leaders constantly explain and elucidate it. Good visions become clouded when leaders can't separate themselves from the issues or become afraid of the consequences the vision demands. Sometimes nothing can fulfill a vision. When a leader or a group lacks resources of competence, nothing will save even their grandest vision of the way things might be. Sometimes an organization's structure cannot contain a vision, and it is left to people outside the organization to make the vision reality.[4]

AVOIDING THE PITFALLS

Over the years I have taught leadership courses to thousands of students in two dozen institutions. In those classes I take a strong stand against autocracy as a primary leadership style. To be sure, leadership is situational, and at times a team leader may find it necessary to act alone, but that option rarely applies to the planning process.

Autocratic Centralization

Every management book worth reading recommends cooperative involvement in planning. Vision may be articulated by a single leader simply because he or she has the visibility and perhaps even the responsibility to do so. But it should reflect a consensus of the leadership team, because no powerful person or group of stakeholders should dominate the planning process. God speaks to all His people, not just to pastors, principals, or presidents.

Sloppy Data Collection

Sloppy research corrupts the implementation of vision as badly as careless fingers on the computer keyboard can open the wrong windows. Writing about the relationship of local churches and mission boards, James Engle sees two paradigm shifts late in the twentieth century: from "passive supporting" to "proactive sending," and from isolation into "mission-focused/synergistic" relationships. He says, "The church now takes the Great Commission as more than an auxiliary assignment and makes pro-active commitment to engage in strategic commitment of people and resources."[5] He identifies fifteen components and their differences within the paradigms. The mission-focused paradigm strongly emphasizes partnering between churches and mission boards, with congregations becoming more involved in the process of recruiting, developing, and sending missionaries.[6]

Weak Decision-Making

Decision-making can be a problem in the financial area. Despite the affluence and rampant materialism of the twenty-first-century Western world, most Christian organizations still face budget restrictions. Visionary focus does not require constantly expanding budgets, because ministry effectiveness cannot be measured in terms of dollars. Priorities flow from the mission and extend out into the vision. Sometimes a budget-cutting decision can actually advance the vision, especially if it diverts funds flowing down a dead-end street to some avenue of ministry that offers new vistas of God-given opportunity. As leaders in higher education know, *niche rather than size determines the difference between thriving or surviving.*

In our day people can afford the price of many commodities, but they still search for value—and that applies to ministry as well as automobiles.

Poor Communication

Every effective leader understands the importance of communicating both mission and vision and makes it a priority from the pulpit and in person. The objectives, the agendas for meetings, and the activities of staff and volunteers all aim toward fulfilling the mission and realizing the vision. Communication removes barriers to participation.

Ministry organizations that share information widely and solve problems collaboratively stand a good chance of walking the planning bridge from mission to vision.

Scan the Environment

An eighteen-wheeler is lumbering closer in the right lane, a utility vehicle is coming off the ramp two hundred yards ahead, and space on the highway is getting cramped. It's time to touch the brake pedal! Like good drivers, leaders scan the environment because they know plans are fulfilled not in a vacuum but in response to what's going on all around our ministry. As a leader you cannot afford to be blind to the *process,* hoping that someday the *product* will justify whatever went on along the way. Don't be blindsided by someone coming off the ramp, and don't ram into the car in front of you—scan the environment.

Long-range planning requires advance information. We look at both internal and external assessment to determine what we have done in the past and what we are doing now. External assessment takes a broad view of the neighborhood, community, state, and eventually our nation and the world. Fortunately, scanning the environment is considerably easier in our day with the kind of research available to us at almost all those levels. The science of demographics coupled with the accessibility of data requires only that we hunt down the information we need to paint a picture of the arenas in which we serve.

Revisit the Mission

Frances Hesselbein writes, "At the Drucker Foundation, we review our mission every three years, and refine it if necessary. The Foundation is almost seven years old, and we've revisited and refined our mission twice—not because we couldn't get it right the first time, with Peter Drucker in the room, but because the environment and the needs of our customers had changed."[7]

Almost every helpful management book emphasizes understanding why an organization exists, that is, its mission. Remember, don't confuse *mission* with *vision.* Judith Bardwick puts it this way: "Determining the business of the business is the first step in setting priorities. This is a major leadership responsibility because, without priorities, efforts are splintered and little is achieved. The best leaders get the organization to focus and to become involved only in what matters the most. . . . Achieving the mission against hard odds, hitting stretch targets in the business of the business—this is the glue that holds people together with the commitment to the good of all."[8]

Ban the Hierarchy

Ultimately all our talk about interdependent congregations and the achievements of ministry teams comes to naught as long as a few power-brokers hold all the influence and pull all the strings. Sadly many churches and Christian organizations have not yet learned this lesson. The point is that twenty-first century people do not find comfort in organizational boxes or on a structured chart. Businesses today are calling themselves "learning organizations," a term that should delight churches everywhere. To quote Hesselbein again, "A round globe now requires round thinking. Forget the top and bottom; think about the center and what spins out from it. Levels? We probably can't get rid of them. But rather than seeing yourself at the top of the org chart, envision yourself at the center of a whirling set of concentric circles. I know, the imagery of 'being at the center' is incongruous with dispersed authority, but it beats 'see you at the top.' "[9]

Disperse the Authority

As stated earlier, leadership should be distributed among the people. Whether we use the words *influence, power,* or *authority,* the principle is the same: *The only way we empower other people is by giving them some of ours.*

Challenge the Process

As Kouzes and Posner noted, effective leaders challenge the process. This doesn't mean they are to be rebellious. Nor does it mean criticizing the behavior of the congregation. Instead it means continuously and unrelentingly asking, "Is there a better way to do this?" We achieve goals when we are willing to make adjustments along the way that enable the process to move ahead more competently and comfortably.

Communicate the Message

"The leader of the future does not sit on the fence, waiting to see which way the wind is blowing. The leader articulates clear positions on issues affecting the organization and is the embodiment of the enterprise, of its values and its principles. Leaders model desired behaviors, never break a promise, and know that leadership is a matter of how to be, not how to do it."[10]

We can't help being drawn to the warmth of Robert Greenleaf's work, especially today when outrageously remunerated cooperative executives line their own and their stockholders' pockets at the expense of thousands of working men and women. In a day of greed Greenleaf called for generosity. In a day of stressful change he argued for "gradualism," by which he meant taking opportunities when they come, a significant idea in ministry planning.

I close this chapter with some of Greenleaf's thought-provoking words.

I use the word *lead* as it is commonly defined: *go out ahead to show the way.* To me, *lead* stands in sharp contrast to *guide, direct, manage,* or *administer.* Because these words imply either *maintenance* (keeping things as they are), *coercion* (sanctions or implied threat of sanctions to enforce one's will), or *manipulation* (guiding others into thoughts or actions that they may not fully understand). As I use the word *lead* it involves creative adventure and risk (as contrasted with maintenance) and it is as free as humanly possible from any implication of coercion or manipulation. Those who follow do so voluntarily, because they fully understand and, through understanding, they are *persuaded* that the ideas or courses of action are right for them."[11]

CHAPTER 8
Changing the Game Plan: Intentional Innovation

IN THE 1999 FRENCH OPEN, Martina Hingis, at that time the number-one women's tennis player in the world, faced a revived and reenergized Steffi Graf. Hingis won the first set, and it looked as if all predictions of a sweep might come true. Then Graf changed her techniques, moving from the baseline to the net, a technique that has not marked her long and efficient career. Just a little intentional innovation, probably drawn up rapidly by her coach after the first set, led to relatively easy victories in the next two sets and the French Open championship.

As stated in the previous chapter, James Kouzes and Barry Posner point out that leaders challenge the process. That sets the tone for this chapter about intentional innovation. Leaders constantly ask, "Is there a better way of doing this?" And leaders who challenge the process will discover themselves quite regularly involved in dynamic change.

Experienced leaders know that the hope of influencing change increases to the degree that we understand it. Of course, leaders should not shake things up just to make them different. Nor should we defend the status quo just because "we've always done it that way."

Somewhere between those two extreme points lies carefully and prayerfully designed change, in which we help people disengage from less effective ways and reorient to new ways of doing things. Thus change begins not with implementation but with awareness and understanding.

Everything we have said about servant leadership and team building comes to something of a crisis point when we enter the dynamic process of change. Since organizations are now seen as learning centers, the old argument that churches and Christian organizations have used for years— "We can't move forward because we work with people who are either underpaid or not on the payroll at all"—holds considerably less clout than it used to. Peter Drucker states that volunteers "have expectations, self-confidence, and, above all, a network. And that gives them mobility, which is probably the greatest change in the human condition. A very short time ago, if you were the son of a peasant, you were going to be a peasant. Even in this country, social mobility was almost unknown. Now, every one of the young people I know has his or her resumé in the bottom drawer, which no blue-collar worker ever did."[1]

BIBLICAL BACKGROUND: SILAS

In the first century a young leader in the church of Jerusalem was caught up in the vortex of change. We first encounter Silas in Acts 15 at the Jerusalem Council. The church leaders there sent him, along with Judas Barsabbas, Paul, and Barnabas, back to Antioch to affirm the council's decision on the important question of what Gentiles must do to be saved (Acts 15:22, 30–34).

This humble but important task produced the first great change in the life of Silas, who functioned almost like an attorney delivering an official document. Not only had the council entrusted the scroll to his care for safety and confidentiality, but they also charged him with explaining the nature of the decision and answering any questions the church might raise. The decision itself represented dramatic change. Relocation from Jerusalem to Antioch brought obvious transitional implications, and then Paul chose Silas to accompany him on what we have come to know as Paul's second and third missionary journeys. In Silas we see a trustworthy Christian on whom the church counted to carry out a seemingly menial task with faithfulness and dignity, a multigifted servant who could handle change in his own life and help others adapt to it.

Silas was a leader in the Jerusalem church (15:22), so he no doubt had ministerial responsibilities there before he was asked to be one of the four to travel to Antioch. We can hardly imagine the sights and sounds Silas encountered traveling through Asia Minor and Greece with Paul and the others. Change became a way of life as we see a leader willing to meet the Gentiles on their own ground as comfortably as he blended with the Jewish elders in the Jerusalem church.

This flexibility, this willingness to take whatever God sent (such as the beating in the Philippian jail; 16:22–23), developed readiness to function in something other than a number-one position. God draped Silas with the essential garments of an innovative leader.

Many church members have quietly accepted the idea that the senior pastor always serves as the point man in instigating change. However, innovative ideas more likely arise from other staff members, or in an educational institution, from vice presidents or directors, who not only bring the initial ideas to the table but are usually responsible for carrying them out.

Later in his ministry Silas showed up as Peter's secretary (1 Pet. 5:12), an excellent choice for a letter sent to strangers scattered throughout Pontus, Galatia, Cappadocia, Asia, and Bithynia. Many scholars believe Peter may have originated the content while Silas did the actual writing, so both phraseology and style would be a genuine team effort. The ministry of Silas demonstrates change. Members of a team agree to assist each other in moving toward improvement—better ways of carrying out the ministries God has given us—an improved game plan.

THE CHALLENGE OF CHANGE

Christian leaders need not be entrepreneurs. But they must be people who have a perpetual quest for improvement. Furthermore leaders need not always seek the challenges they face, since often those challenges seek us. Quite likely the greatest challenge of the Jimmy Carter presidency was the Iran hostage crisis, hardly something any president would engineer.

Sometimes young leaders develop a change-agent complex and begin to meddle with things about which they know too little or for which effective change is still several years away. It is a sin to "rearrange" a church's ministries just to show the congregation that we are there and doing something.

Challenge also sets the stage for potential excellence, a goal toward which we must all strive. And we can thank God that challenge, particularly unexpected challenge, often calls for skills and abilities that we didn't know we had until God activated them and required us to use them.

HANDLING RESISTANCE TO CHANGE

The television premier of the cartoon strip *Dilbert* aired on January 25, 1999. In it a product line had gone bad, and the company needed to recoup its losses by coming up with something new. The boss demanded a new product and gave Dilbert the job of handling the first phase of the change—a new name for the product! With typical caricatures and outrageous irony, the program unfolded with Dilbert and Dogbert racing around to come up with a name that would be acceptable to the boss. They had no idea what the product would be, but through a series of typically Dilbertian chaotic events they agreed on "Salmonella." Amazingly the boss decided he liked it and determined the company would probably create a new car to go with the name!

Less ridiculous but far more dangerous by eternity's standards is the pastor who throws a church into turmoil without carefully thinking through the necessity of a change, how best to implement it, and how the leadership team will handle resistance. Let's think for a minute about what happens to people during major change in a Christian organization.

Awkwardness

Many people feel uncomfortable during a change even if they voted to go ahead with it. That awkwardness can come from several sources but arises most often from the way the leadership team approaches the change. Have a look at the words of Peter Senge: "As with any lasting change, the senior executive's ability to implement a true learning organization is overrated. Most people who reach the top of an organization soon find they have little unilateral power to control its complex workings. That reality led the CEO of an international energy company to call the word *drive*—as in 'How do you drive change?'—the most useless word in the language.

'You drive an automobile,' he says. 'You don't drive a human system. If you try, you might end up doing more harm than good.' "[2]

Why can't pastors learn that? How is it that secular consultants dealing with *Fortune 500* companies recognize that the change process moves forward through the development of guiding principles, while some Christian leaders think they can best accomplish it by clever politics or even secretive manipulation? What can we do to create an environment in which people willingly open their minds to new and better ways of doing ministry? We can only articulate new strategies after the leadership team has agreed to take responsibility to see them through. In my opinion we become arrogant and even sinfully abusive when we bang people's heads against our own ideas until they either submissively follow what we want or leave the church. The way some leaders handle change, *awkward* probably doesn't adequately describe how a congregation feels.

Loss

When the game plan changes, people tend to focus on what they have lost, not what they will gain. The greater the change, the greater the loss. We need not argue about whether that response is good or bad, mature or immature—we need only recognize its reality. If we begin to sing only praise choruses from slides on a screen or wall, people have *lost* the hymnal and, more importantly, hundreds of years of theological hymnody. If we lock up the organ and bring on the worship team guitars, people have *lost* something they loved. So we need to be careful here. These sentences offer no value judgment; they simple describe how people feel. And these examples are mere tokens; you can fill in a dozen more from your own experience.

The fact that we have seen enormous change in the second half of the twentieth century does not alleviate the feeling of loss. The accelerated sales of rap music (11 percent higher in 1998 over the previous year) does absolutely nothing to mitigate a person's *loss* of Glenn Miller and Nat King Cole on 95 percent of the radio stations in any major city.

You may call it nostalgia, being old-fashioned, stodginess, or whatever you wish. But as a leader you can't ignore the issue of loss in people's response to change. And we ought not associate change resistance with age. A teenager no more wants to give up his boom box or baggy jeans than the oldest member of your congregation wants to lose choir robes or dignity in the service.

Fear

Since change almost always takes us into the unknown, people sense a certain amount of fear attached to it, even among those who favor the new plan. They fear a number of things, such as the timing of the change or what appears to them a lack of resources to make it possible. Peter Koestenbaum puts it this way: "Beyond change and the acceleration of change, there is the *direction* of change, and that is uncertain. Life and work are a series of capricious frustrations and arbitrary surprises. One cannot be adequately prepared for the unexpected, which nevertheless is certain to occur."[3]

To calm such fears, good ministry coaches emphasize spiritual peace and prayer. They talk often and openly about change, keep the goals in clear focus, and relate everything to the organization's mission. They communicate frequently. They help people raise their capacity for change and thereby help them adjust their attitudes.

Intolerance

Few attitudes are less tolerated in our contemporary culture than intolerance. But this becomes the final trench of resistance, the point at which people dig in their heels and refuse to take another step. But genuine servant leaders can rush to the rescue. People intolerant of change can be brushed aside or told they can "either get with the program or leave." The record of many churches in sacrificing the few for the good of the many is nothing less than appalling.

Or, with loving patience, we can trust God to overcome the awkwardness, loss, and fear without which people lose their basis for intolerance. Doug Murren offers good advice: "Be humble. Don't be a know-it-all. Granted, a leader must have confidence in the plans proposed, but a truly great leader acknowledges that he does not know everything and cannot perfectly predict the outcomes of new strategies. Sometimes the best thing you can do in response to those who are harshly critical of your innovative ideas is to ask them to allow your idea a chance to fail. Rather than boldly predicting a smashing success, simply say, 'Let's see if it will work.' "[4]

After we gather ideas from every source (especially the leadership team), we focus on priorities and handle the process with great care. We honor risk-taking and even model it. We foster hardiness, courage, and patience throughout the congregation. And we keep our priorities in line with the mission.

Common Coping Reactions

Doug Rumford reminds leaders to "honor the past." This is sound advice. When people really believe that you affirm the heritage of the congregation and love its history, people may trust you with its future. Rumford tells an interesting story: "One pastor put a roll of newsprint on the walls around the fellowship hall. On it he drew a time line of the congregation's existence and encouraged members to fill in significant events in the life of the church. They scribbled the smallest to the greatest events. It became a tangible expression of God's goodness, which generated new enthusiasm to see God work again. It also communicated that the new pastor respected their history."[5]

But even when we do that, even when we gently and patiently guard the change process, groups tend to employ certain strategies to cope with the new game plan. Note the difference here. Earlier we were discussing how *individuals* respond; now we want to take a look at how *groups* congeal not just to resist change, but also to handle it, that is, to cope.

Hang On to the Past

Falling back on the familiar is common behavior for all of us. When driving through a strange city at peak traffic hours, it's easier to stay with the interstate than to try to wander around a series of one-way streets. Most people find it hard to throw away a really comfortable pair of old slippers or even trade in a car or truck that has served them well for many years.

And the past is not bad or wrong just because it's older than the present or the future. The nation of Israel preserved itself through seventy years of captivity by clinging tenaciously to its theology and traditions—by holding on to the past. So, as Rumford has suggested, wise leaders link the past with the future, celebrating both and emphasizing their connection. The early Christians did not discard the Old Testament simply because there was now a New Testament. When people corporately hold on to the past, we should neither rebuke them nor shun them. We celebrate with them and together realize how the past has become a gateway to the future, a bridge to tomorrow.

See Change as Threat

Many people feel that change is a shock, a threat to the known and the familiar. Yet change is viewed as less of a threat when the trust factor is present. That is, leaders who have served their ministries for long periods of time, and served them well, have built up a trust account for times of change. *Trust mitigates threat, which begins to subside when people see leaders translate personal integrity into organizational fidelity.*

Accelerate Present Ministries

Sometimes groups threatened by change simply do more of the same—faster, harder, and better. They reasonably (though often incorrectly) conclude that they may be losing some treasured activity or structure because they did not do it well enough. But the real question in ministry is not how well we do something (though we should value competence highly), but whether a given program or service reflects and achieves the mission. I like the way Douglas Smith puts it: "Too often, change efforts produce a bifurcated reality: You've got the business and you've got the change. Well, guess which one gets short shrift? The change. *Only when you challenge people to deliver performance outcomes that are relevant to their mission can you engage them in the change process. . . .* Your goals have to focus on tangible performance, not just activity. So it's not a matter of sending people to training sessions on continuous improvement, having them read books on continuous improvement, or benchmarking your competitors. You have to let people learn by doing and performing, and then provide the help they need to perform."[6]

Join in the Planning Process

This is our goal from the beginning—to get people involved. When Christian leaders wear a change-agent badge, they sometimes create a negative "us and them" mentality. So we should dump the term "change agent" in favor of something more team-friendly such as "facilitator" or "helper." People on whom we depend to make innovation or improvement should be involved in the process from the beginning.

KEYS TO EFFECTIVE CHANGE

In recent years reliable secular writers have argued that the traditional or "heroic" model of leadership is hopelessly outdated. People who insist on calling all the shots and naming all the changes squander the talents of others and stifle team creativity. Dayton Fandray writes, "It's not enough to tell your employees that you value their input if you're still making the tough decisions by yourself. They may give you honest advice based on rigorous analysis, or they may tell you whatever it is they think you want to hear. Either way, they know it will be you who ultimately shoulders responsibility for the decision. When responsibility is shared, however, the distinction between manager and subordinate blurs. Yes, the manager will ultimately be held accountable for all decisions, both good and bad. And, yes, there will be times when the manager will find it necessary to overrule decisions made by the group. But in the long run, decisions *will* be based on consensus."[7]

So leadership style sets the stage for effective innovation. But what are the keys, the steps in the process?

Make Plain How the Change Facilitates Organizational Goals

Assuming that your people understand the objectives of the organization (and that may be a major assumption), any change in the functions or form of the organization should clearly relate back to stated objectives. In the educational cycle one constantly evaluates on the basis of educational objectives. Conceivably the objectives might change, or, more commonly, our understanding of how the objectives may best be achieved will change. Regular evaluation may require restructuring in the organization.

People will change more rapidly, with more positive results, when they understand how any innovation will enhance rather than obscure the fulfillment of purposes with which they agree.

Create a Positive Climate for Change

Many leaders run into difficulty with change, primarily because they stand up to bat with two strikes against them. Hostility and a ferment of dissatisfaction pervade the organization, and the announcement of change becomes the *coup de grace* in that leadership union. To bring back a happy climate in an organization, some leaders attempt "bargaining" for the change. But that can lead to an obstinacy on both sides and a win-lose approach to final decisions.

At least three factors can help create a positive climate. The first is the *process of "unfreezing."* We apply this term primarily to the creation of dissatisfaction with the status quo. To put it more simply, people have to be somewhat unhappy with the present game plan before they will welcome a new one. "God's frozen people" have to be thawed a bit, and, as with most thawing processes, this one is best accomplished through warm leadership.

Second is our own *nonjudgmental attitudes.* Leaders tend to react negatively when someone opposes their plans or programs. But frigid reaction to resisters can never facilitate the thawing process. If we condemn our opponents, common ice cubes could change into dry ice and doom all prospects of change.

Third, we build a base of *support through diplomacy.* Too many leaders try to win battles on the open floor of a committee or board meeting, thinking that pure democracy demands oratorical defense of every issue. But things do not often get done that way. Jesus constantly discussed matters with His disciples. He planted pieces of information and seed thoughts for ideas which He hoped would blossom in a future day. This is what we should do with key people in the organization. And as already suggested, this should occur *before* we announce the change.

We reduce resistance to change when we reach an agreement on the extent of change, the rate of change, and the style of implementation. This strongly implies that even the planning stage should utilize a number of people, and that is precisely the next point.

Involve People at All Levels in the Change Process

Individual group members in isolation (even leaders) have limited effect without the wholehearted cooperation of the rest of the group. Research shows that we can better obtain such cooperation by letting people have a larger "piece of the action." Sometimes the best thing that can happen to a new idea is to give it away and make it group property.

In the same way that groups can thwart change, they can facilitate it. We want as many people on our side of the net as possible before the match begins. Participation depends on the sincerity and honesty with which we go about attempts to involve other people. This is not tokenism; it is a genuine commitment to team leadership.

Begin at the Point of Most Control

Some leaders go awry because they reach beyond any effective grasp to produce innovative procedures. Most of us find it easier to whisper to someone close to us than to shout at someone two blocks away. All of us have a particular point of reference in which we have greater authority. A worship leader, for example, who wants to see some genuine renewal in a church would be unwise to start recommending changes in the missions program. He should begin with worship, his point of most influence.

Yanked from his roots in Jerusalem, Silas was sent scurrying across Asia Minor trying to keep up with the apostle Paul. Even when Silas was imprisoned for his faith, Silas never gave off the aura of a victim. Yet many leaders look exactly that way when their strenuous efforts at innovation fail. A victim mentality leads to fear, frustration, whining, complaining, and stress. Victims blame other people for their problems and see no way out of the difficulties others have caused them. Price Pritchett and Ron Pound put it this way: "Any time we act like a victim, we actually weaken ourselves. We load ourselves down with more self-induced stress. Beyond that, we set ourselves up as an even more likely candidate for future victimization, because we literally make ourselves more expendable. Our public suffering makes us much less appealing as an employee."[8]

The solution to victimization lies not in control but in confidence— confidence in God's call and His plan for your life in ministry, confidence in the team members you have placed around you to share ministry burdens and press forward with vision. You can be confident that your effectiveness does not rest in the number of people who agree with you but in your gentle, meek, wise, and mature handling of change.

CHAPTER 9
Give It Your Best: Quality Control

A FEW YEARS AGO a major news magazine conducted a survey among people it considered "distinguished Americans," asking them to rate thirty institutions according to their effect on decisions influencing the nation. On that list, ranked highest to lowest, positions twenty-four, twenty-five, and twenty-six were occupied by education, family, and church. In these days when everyone speaks about the culture wars and postmodernity, it may be worth reminding ourselves that what we celebrate as Christians is not our social or political impact on North American or global society. We celebrate what God has done through his pilgrims and strangers, who have always had a relatively insignificant impact on the wider culture of the secular world.

Yet that impact, however small and inconsequential by the world's standards, must be carried out at a level of excellence that brings glory to God. Ministries that are centered in the absolute truth of the Bible make possible the "learning organization" we call church. Let's never forget that our commitment to absolute truth forms the major distinction between Christian thinking and secular thinking.

The phrase Total Quality Management (TQM) originated with W. Edward Deming, the author of eight technical books and almost two hundred scholarly studies. His works on quality, productivity, and competitive position form the foundation for our understanding of TQM. The work of Deming (and the concept of TQM) is less popular now than ten years ago, but the principle of doing one's work with excellence and of practicing quality control in ministry cannot be minimized. The thrust of this chapter, therefore, is to cast Deming's general concepts of quality in the more contemporary framework of cutting-edge leadership thinking today.

BIBLICAL BACKGROUND: TIMOTHY

In 1 and 2 Timothy, Paul, a veteran and senior elder in the church, instructed young Timothy regarding his life and ministry in the congregation at Ephesus.

Eavesdropping on the personal conversation of one pastor to another, we discover Paul's heart for Timothy and his congregation. He urged Timothy and his flock to be involved in ministry. He stressed that ministry is for all believers, not just the pastor. In the biblical sense we are all ministers, and Paul's words of instruction and exhortation to Timothy bring us encouragement and benefit as well. They propel us to work toward excellence in all our ministry efforts.

Enemies of the Truth

All his life Paul fought against legalism. Some legalists stayed within the boundaries of the church and attacked the apostle from a position of rigid traditionalism. Others wandered off into various forms of false doctrine and tried to turn the Old Testament Law against Paul and his preaching of freedom in the gospel of Christ. The false teachers mentioned in 1 Timothy 1:3–4 may have been nominal members of the congregation at Ephesus. Whatever their relation to the church, they corrupted God's pure grace by mixing it with false doctrine.

Like the circumcision crowd that plagued the church in Jerusalem (Acts 15), these "Law teachers" wanted to put Christians under the full jurisdiction of the Law. They had missed the truth and turned aside to substitutes.

All this promoted "controversies rather than God's work" (1 Tim. 1:4), a disease certainly not unknown in the modern church. Biblical preaching and teaching, then as now, present the pure gospel of God's grace in

Christ and call forth a response of faith and love. When people accept the gospel, they do so because they see themselves as lost and are drawn to Christ. Spiritual growth then leads to a "pure heart," "a good conscience," and "sincere [literally, 'unhypocritical'] faith" (1:5).

Danger to the Truth

What purpose does the Law serve? It was given, for one thing, to control lawbreakers, rebels, ungodly and sinful people, unholy and irreligious people, murderers, adulterers, perverts, slave traders, and liars (1:8–10). Quite a list! Some commentators believe that Paul may have had the Ten Commandments in mind here as he listed these flagrant sins. Several observations seem warranted: (1) Rebellion is as sinful as lawbreaking. (2) Profane behavior, the crude and lewd lifestyles of many modern people, can clearly be labeled ungodly, sinful, and unholy. (3) Sexual perversion, such as homosexuality, ranks right up there with adultery. (4) Slave trading is not just a social injustice; it is a blatant sin, linked here with lying.

The Law points up the sinfulness of behaviors. But to bring the Law into the church at Ephesus (or anywhere else) as a guide for Christians is to miss the purpose of both law and grace. Christians have something far better: the Holy Spirit, who continually guides from within, and the New Covenant, which describes proper patterns of life. Only when sound theology anchors consistent spiritual growth can we turn our attention to quality control in ministry.

COMMITMENTS TO QUALITY MINISTRY

I once read about a physicians' banquet in which the guest speaker was scheduled to address the topic "Emergency Medicine." One of the guests choked on a piece of food during dinner and died because not one doctor in the room could correctly administer the Heimlich maneuver. The story seems a bit far-fetched, but the point should grab every church. Competence to carry out ministry must characterize our congregations. We must make a collective commitment to give it our best.

Commitment to Integrated Thinking

Christian leaders hold a mandate to bring people to maturity, to spiritual adulthood, to a place at which they are no longer tossed about nor indecisive about the foundations of their faith (Eph. 4:13–15). We must determine what Christian maturity looks like, and how and where integrated thinking skills fit into that maturity. We teach people to think through what makes ministry effective. We challenge people to design better programs, organization, and ministries that will attract others in new and more dynamic ways. To do that we tap into creative thinking, throwing out old boundaries and approaching our challenges from a fresh perspective, asking questions that penetrate to the root of our mission and give impetus for an expanded vision.

Commitment to Public Reputation

In 1 Timothy 3:2–12 Paul identified numerous qualifications for church elders and deacons. These lists reveal the fact that we should not take lightly the business of serving the Lord. To serve as a church leader is a deep responsibility and an enormous challenge. Church leaders, Paul indicated, must have a reputation of integrity with the world, with those in the church whom they would lead, and with God Himself. Quality ministry is to be carried out by quality people known in the church and the community as true followers of the Lord.

Commitment to Cooperative Ministry

When a Christian organization pushes teamwork, it does not necessarily buy into a secular business concept; rather, it affirms a basic biblical truth. Romans 12:5 reminds us that believers are united in Christ. "So in Christ we who are many form one body, and each member belongs to all the others." Why then do we applaud the lone ranger who builds a large church on the strength of his own personality? Why do we repeatedly affirm Christian superstars and ignore the millions who live out their faith day by day? Why do we accentuate competition in ministry rather than urging cooperation and teamwork? When Christians learn to help each other, to make up for their own weaknesses with another's strength, they reflect the unity Christ desires of us.

Commitment to the Guiding Mission

The importance of an organization's mission cannot be overemphasized. As stated earlier, mission represents the purpose of a ministry, and vision is a picture of its future. A third component—values—describes how we intend to behave as we carry out the mission and pursue the vision. But there's a catch here, and Peter Senge describes it well. "There is a big difference between having a mission statement and being truly mission-based. To be truly mission-based means that key decisions can be referred to the mission—our reason for being. It means that people can and should object to management edicts that they do not see as connected to the mission. It means that thinking about and continually clarifying the mission is everybody's job. . . . In most organizations no one would dream of challenging a management decision on the grounds that it does not serve the mission. In other words, most organizations serve those in power rather than a mission."[1]

Commitment to Courageous Experimentation

We all know failure breeds success, since we learn so much from creative mistakes. Every church ought to be building an environment that frees its people to discover new approaches to ministry and new solutions to constantly changing problems. Ministry organizations whose departments or divisions work at cross-purposes drain incentive for fresh ideas. Such a climate promotes lack of solidarity, rather than global or holistic thinking, and can quickly degenerate into turf protection.

Quality control in ministry remains an unreachable goal without wide-angle thinking. Edward Deming repeatedly emphasizes the need to have the "big picture" in mind. He reminds us that "the only way to change or improve an organization is to view it as a whole and implement changes throughout the entire system."[2]

CHECKLIST FOR QUALITY MINISTRY

On any given day 4,885 AAA members are locked out of their cars. AAA receives 1,783,000 calls annually and reminds its members to remove their keys when they exit and keep one in a billfold or purse. Good idea. Our grandparents taught us that an ounce of prevention is worth a pound of cure. Let's apply that to protecting the quality of ministry. Leaving ministry in disrepair because no one notices or understands the concept of excellence may represent the worst scenario. But only slightly less desirable is a leadership style that constantly practices crisis management, dealing with broken ministries and broken people after the fact. How can we build in safeguards up front?

Clear Mission

Edward Deming calls this "constancy of purpose" and emphasizes something we all know, namely, that many organizations that have a mission statement rarely consult it. And this results in a string of ministries unrelated or only loosely related to the mission. Major managerial processes such as long-range planning, goal achievement, and management of change are inseparably related to the mission. The more fuzzy and obscure the mission, the more oblique the vision and the strategies.

Competent Management

Though leadership and management are two distinct things, in ministry we can hardly separate the two. Good coaches do not tell players what to do and then punish them if they don't do it; they coach. Coaching consists of helping people do a better job, learning by experience how to increase ministry quality. And part of effective coaching is recognizing and thanking team members who do well.

Cooperative Attitudes

Deming urges us to "drive out fear" and to "break down barriers between staff areas."[3] This is good advice for any church. Too many congregants are afraid to ask questions or seek help even when they do not understand how a ministry works. The result is that people continue to do things ineffectively or do not do them at all. To perform with quality, people need to feel secure in their ministries.

Too often boards and staffs compete between or among themselves, depleting precious resources. When one segment of a ministry team causes problems for another, we can almost feel quality diminishing.

Constant Improvement

In secular organizations the phrase "constant improvement" refers to product enhancement or tweaking the techniques of marketing. In a church it more likely centers on what some would call "small wins," incremental steps toward higher quality in our ministry programs. According to David and Mark Nadler, "Organizational learning doesn't just happen—top leadership has to make it happen. There are informal ways to support learning that involves the way leaders treat risk-takers who don't always succeed, but learning can also be formalized. . . . The object isn't to criticize or lay blame; instead, senior executives—sometimes the CEO—make it clear from the outset that the only objective is to learn from experience, so lessons can be applied appropriately throughout the company."[4]

Correct Targets

Focusing on correct targets offers a desperately needed corrective for many churches—eliminate numerical quotas. Edward Deming talks about an airline reservations clerk under a directive to answer twenty-five calls an hour, while being courteous and not rushing callers. "Sometimes the computer is slow in providing information. Sometimes it is entirely unresponsive and she must resort to directories and guides. Yet there is no leeway in the twenty-five-call mandate. What is her job? To take twenty-five calls or to satisfy the customer? She cannot do both."[5]

Too many churches operate with "total quantity management." We number everything from attendance at the morning service to the missions offering. Then we measure success by rising numbers. Yet the biblical "bottom line" has very little to do with numbers of any kind—it deals rather with the quality of living and loving displayed in the body of Christ that makes it attractive to unbelievers.

Components of Quality Ministry

Sometime ago I picked up a bulletin in a church where I was preaching on a Sunday morning and noticed a listing of the multiple staff by their titles—senior pastor, youth director, and others. In that same list appeared the word "ministers" in the plural, and after it the words "the entire congregation."

That is certainly biblical! The genius of the New Testament rests in lay leadership, which lies at the heart of the Bible's distinct philosophy of ministry. Timothy was a team player, working with Paul in ministry, a disciple or learner charged with the responsibility to teach others. "Command and teach these things. Don't let anyone look down on you because you are young, but set an example for the believers in speech, in life, in love, in faith and in purity. Until I come, devote yourself to the public reading of Scripture, to preaching and to teaching. Do not neglect your gift, which was given you through a prophetic message when the body of elders laid their hands on you" (1 Tim. 4:11–14).

Timothy was perhaps in his midthirties when he read those words, and in the first century such an influential position would not normally be held by a man so young. For that reason some had apparently called his appointment into question. Timothy himself had obviously underrated his own ability and position in the church, so Paul encouraged him to use the spiritual gifts God had given him.

Every church leader should be a model in speech, life, love, faith, and purity. Some have suggested that Timothy had a nonassertive personality, and they have criticized that leadership style. Even if that was true of Timothy, we should never confuse meekness with weakness, especially in serving the Lord.

The following four items serve only as thought-prompters; you may add others as you customize this book to your own ministry needs. The four I have chosen are components in which I see room for learning and improving the quality.

Quality in preaching. The familiar challenge from Paul jumps out at us from the early verses of 2 Timothy: "In the presence of God and of Christ Jesus, who will judge the living and the dead, and in view of his appearing and his kingdom, I give you this charge: Preach the Word" (2 Tim. 4:1–2). Yet unfortunately many churches have all but eliminated the exposition of the Scriptures. Becoming specialists in management and marketing, some pastors lose sight of this central component, which cries out for excellence and the highest of quality.

Quality in nurture. In everything from an early-childhood Sunday-school class to an in-depth Bible study for adults we must upgrade our learning systems.[6] Training and experience are the two rails on which the train of nurture moves forward—that is, our church educational ministries improve in quality as we provide training for our workers and give them experience in ministry.

Quality in relationships. Few congregations in our day split over doctrine; church fights much more commonly develop over relationships. Teaching believers how to live in love and unity can lead to significant progress in our quest for quality. The following paragraph from Paul's letter to the church at Philippi, if fully obeyed, could bring revival to some congregations almost overnight: "If you have any encouragement from being united with Christ, if any comfort from his love, if any fellowship with the Spirit, if any tenderness and compassion, then make my joy complete by being like-minded, having the same love, being one in spirit and purpose. Do nothing out of selfish ambition or vain conceit, but in humility consider others better than yourselves. Each of you should look not only to your own interests, but also to the interests of others. Your attitude should be the same as that of Christ Jesus" (Phil. 2:1–5).

Quality in family life. Many Americans look to public education to build in the moral values no longer taught at home—but they look in vain. Intellectual development does not necessarily lead to integrity and morality. By God's design the family affords the central focus for moral and spiritual development. Nevertheless God has placed families in the larger family we call "church," and that larger family succeeds in its mission insofar as it enables individual families to carry out their mission. A megachurch may offer more program options to a larger array of demographic groups, but that does not necessarily improve the quality of its ministry to families. Churches must stand in partnership with parents. And the greater that partnership in promoting the spiritual nurture of our children and young people, the closer we will move toward excellence in ministry.

Quality control in ministry calls for us to think critically about our ministries and ways of doing things. Christian organizations must cultivate the ability to identify and challenge assumptions, to imagine and explore alternatives, while evaluating tentative conclusions against the standards of God's Word. When defining absolutes, we would do well to follow the model of Jesus and to trust the Holy Spirit to lead us into truth. Such an environment can provide an opportunity for Spirit-generated quality, the hallmark of ministry with excellence.

CHAPTER 10
After the Starting Gun: Empowering Others

In what we commonly call "micromanaging," leaders get their grip on an organization or congregation and, like a giant octopus, stretch their tentacles throughout all its activities. No decision can be made, no activity planned, no meetings held without the presence or permission of "the boss." When that type of leader is particularly good, he or she can demonstrate a certain amount of efficiency within limited boundaries. But effectiveness eludes such a style, and other people do not develop into leaders.

Micromanaging involves a lot of "managing" but only small doses of leadership. Power is evident, but empowerment is nearly nonexistent. C. William Pollard, chairman of the ServiceMaster Company, writes, "As groups of different people work together under effective leaders, we are confronted with the reality that no one person can accomplish the task alone. An individual standing alone contributes less than he or she does as a member of the whole."[1]

Track is a team sport even though it does not always appear that way. In a relay race, for example, four runners depend on each other with only a split second of contact, and the coach depends on all of them without any hands-on control after the starting gun. That's what this chapter is about—sharing responsibility and authority with other people. Call it delegation or empowerment, the process is essentially the same. And it began centuries ago, long before the American Management Association held its first meeting.

BIBLICAL BACKGROUND: JETHRO

Exodus 18 offers one of the most important chapters in the entire Bible on the subject of administrative leadership. It pictures Moses and his host of exiles just recently separated from Egypt and getting settled in the wilderness. Jethro, priest of Midian, paid a visit to his son-in-law. The recent development was something Jethro had never anticipated during Moses' forty years of living with the family in Midian.

We know very little about Jethro—he was apparently a wise man and probably a believer in God. Jethro could have had contact with the Lord through the line of Midian, son of Abraham by Keturah (Gen. 25:1–2). Exodus 18:7–26 seems to suggest that Moses welcomed his father-in-law, thought highly of his advice, and immediately implemented his suggestion.

It took wise Jethro just one glance to discover that Moses' system would never do. His words are a classic statement of the meaning of delegation: "You and these people who come to you will only wear yourselves out. The work is too heavy for you; you cannot handle it alone" (18:18).

Moses was overburdened by his failure to delegate, and that in turn minimized leadership development among the people. One management periodical states the issue clearly: "Lack of people qualified for delegation and greater responsibilities can rarely be blamed on others. Your help in many ways to encourage an employee's growth will not only help you to get your work done but help with an attitude which will motivate him to want to give greater assistance. This obviously requires time—but there's great payoff to every one related to the company."[2]

The carefully constructed organizational package that Jethro proposed hardly resembled bureaucracy in any sophisticated sense. He clearly provided for the flow of communication. People who needed access to Moses could still see him—and now without waiting three or four days in the hot desert sun.

Jethro noted that if God commended his advice and Moses implemented it, then there would be harmony and peace in the camp (18:23). Moses apparently considered this the will of God and put the plan into operation.

BASIC INGREDIENTS

Micromanaging too often leads to manipulation. We manipulate people when we use some devious means to influence their thinking or behavior in a way that serves our own purposes. Sometimes we use guilt, sometimes fear, sometimes any means available. While it may work, it is almost always wrong.

People bring a variety of needs and motives into a ministry situation, and we know they are motivated by a sense of achievement, even a sense of competence in what they do. And when we have the right people in the right places, we must empower them and release them for ministry achievement.

What does it take to let go of ministry control so others can blossom? Certainly treating people (not money, machines, or minds) as our greatest resource may be the key, but several attitudes and behaviors—flexibility, communication, accountability, training—help us use that key in the right doors at the right times.

Flexibility

Micromanagers tend to be rigid people, requiring others to do things the way they would do them. They don't share ministry gladly; they don't help people work together; they don't appeal to internal motivation. Team leaders, on the other hand, relate to others and bend the boundaries of the organization so that people can fit into ministry opportunities for which God has gifted them. They take as much delight in the achievements of a volunteer as they do their own accomplishments. Pollard describes the atmosphere at ServiceMaster. "First, we seek to recognize the dignity and worth of all people because they have been created in God's image. Thus, our role as leaders involves more than just what people do on the job. We also must be involved in what they are becoming as whole people and how the work environment is contributing to the process. Are these people growing as individuals who can contribute at work, at home, and in the community?"[3]

Japanese managerial experts often compare leadership to air, considering it necessary for life but impossible to see or touch. By comparison, we are told, American bosses seem brash and bullying. Japanese leaders tend to climb the corporate ranks by performance and then lead by consensus rather than command. Words like "our" replace "my" and "mine." I find it interesting that Christian leaders who complain that congregations resist change seem so rigid in their own leadership styles. Letting go of ministry control requires flexibility.

Communication

The more one works with untrained volunteers, the more important communication becomes. And here's the catch—because information is power, leaders tend to hold on to it, operating in a military style on a "need-to-know" basis. Yet in most churches, people *need to know* much more than they do—more about the Bible, theology, ministry skills, and other concerns. A commitment to flexibility requires a commitment to communication so that people can be empowered by knowledge to function in the learning organization we call "church."

And let's not forget the listening dimension of communication. Doug Burrell discusses this. "Listening is a powerful and too-often-unused tool of ministry. Think about physicians for a moment. All their knowledge of medicine and the human body, all their experience with other patients, and all their research and knowledge of the latest in medicine are useless until they listen to you tell what ails you. Should a doctor say, 'I've seen enough patients now to know what you need,' would you feel comfortable? The power and importance of listening in ministry is no less important. A failure to listen is a failure in professional responsibility."[4]

Accountability

So much well-meaning delegation goes awry at this point. *In accountability we do not let go of people, we let go of power.* When we delegate both responsibility and authority, we still have the responsibility to maintain accountability, holding people to achieve what they agreed to do.

I always encourage lay leaders to serve publicly in the Sunday morning worship service. Let's assume that a senior pastor has asked an elder or deacon to read the Scripture on a given Sunday. Fifteen minutes before the service the man can't be found. The pastor discovers that he left town on a fishing trip for the weekend. Whether the absence can be attributed to carelessness or poor communication, the pastor has to follow through to ensure that that kind of behavior doesn't happen again. Olan Hendrix writes, "The leader who is delegating is solely responsible to elicit accountability from the volunteer to whom the task has been given, remembering that work relationships with volunteers need to be handled with a great deal of sensitivity. The leader must learn to elicit accountability in the way that will cause the volunteer to grow and derive satisfaction from the performance of the task."[5]

Training

Once new leaders have been located and recruited, they become members of the team. Now we coach them to play the game, using the right signals and plays so they will not have to spend too much time on the bench. Precisely at this point many leaders make a serious recruitment mistake. They work hard on a prospect until he or she gives a yes answer and then rush off to some other task, leaving that person to find out what to do and how to do it.

Three specific elements form the foundation of an effective leadership training program: *motivation, standards,* and *evaluation.*

Motivation is essential to the effective functioning of any organization. If an organization has proper goals, leaders focus on these and the mission. To put it another way, we ought to take a human-resources view of leadership training. New leaders must not only be taught how to put round pegs in round holes, but they should also be encouraged to develop a total view of how they fit into the work of the overall ministry.

Performance standards explain precisely what we expect of people in the organization and what they may expect of us. We often hear the complaints, "I'm not sure that's my responsibility," or, "I never know how well I am doing my job." Both these attitudes lead to insecurity and frustration on the part of new leaders, and so we should encourage the opposite attitudes as early as possible.

Good leaders emphasize both the total objectives of the organization and the importance of fitting personal goals into them. What *you* have learned to do, you now teach to promising leaders. As they identify with ministry objectives, they learn to fit into the total perspective. Trust and respect make it possible to establish and enforce ministry standards. We want new leaders to be a part of that climate and to foster the spirit of cooperation which we have tried to build.

Evaluation must follow motivation and standards. When we agree to a leadership post, we agree to evaluate the work of others and to give them some kind of "grade" on their levels of performance. We particularly evaluate new leaders brought into the organization. Much of our review and appraisal of coworkers will be subjective, forming judgments on the basis of what we see and hear rather than on a formal rating form.

Sometimes the trainee can be asked to complete a written evaluation form. This can measure how well he thinks he has accomplished his goals and fulfilled your expectations for him. This usually leads to a personal interview in which you can learn a great deal about your new leader's problems and strengths.

Effective leaders who reject micromanagement set high standards and don't "dumb down" their expectations of ministry performance. They flex, they communicate, they hold people accountable, they train, and they evaluate. They trust people and expect them to serve God with excellence. They radiate what Alfred DeCrane calls "an appreciation of the principle that well-informed team members are the most motivated and strongest achievers, with a willingness to communicate with teams and to follow through."[6]

ESSENTIAL QUALITIES

I have often heard Howard Hendricks say that if Moses came down from the mountain today, the tablets he would carry would be aspirin. Few thinking people deny the reality of confusion, even chaos, that pervades today's world. Surely part of that must be attributed to the fact that we have denied and renounced God's order in our personal lives, in our homes, in our churches, and in society at large. Many people calling themselves Christians have rejected God's claim on their lives for a distinctive Christian lifestyle and meaningful ministry.

Christian leaders who want to cut others loose to thrive in ministry step out of that chaos and into a new and perhaps uncomfortable role. When we make this kind of commitment we allow God to clothe us with qualities we want others to emulate. What are those essential qualities in team leadership?

Alertness

According to an old legend a prophet entered a city to cry against its sins. "Power, greed, and corruption," he shouted in the marketplace. "Power, greed, and corruption." At first people were arrested by his boldness and the obvious sincerity of his message. They stopped to listen—but rarely to heed. As he continued to cry, the crowds grew smaller until he found himself standing alone but still shouting, "Power, greed, and corruption." One of the citizens approached him and asked, "Why do you still shout out your message? Isn't it obvious no one listens?" "At first," the prophet responded, "I shouted to change this city. Now I shout so they will not change me."

Effective leaders stay alert to things happening around them. They also stay alert to what's going on within them, intentionally and continuously engaging in exacting self-evaluation. In order to plow our way back to the biblical concept of the crucified Christ and the self-denying Christian, we tear off the outer garments society has placed on us and pray that God will not allow us to become callous to our culture.

Alertness also requires that we be protected from hyperactivity. In ministry, as in any other worthy endeavor, activity is no substitute for productivity. In these days of militant politics one wonders how the world sees the church to which Jesus once said, "All men will know that you are my disciples, if you love one another" (John 13:35). We must avoid the kind of evaluation that measures success in terms of carnal criteria rather than biblical basics.

Meekness

However large the corporation, the board names only one chief executive officer. Whether we consider ourselves "management" or not, that internal alertness we talked about should turn us toward humility. Paul wrote to the Corinthians these poignant words: "Brothers, think of what you were when you were called. Not many of you were wise by human standards; not many were influential; not many were of noble birth. But God chose the foolish things of the world to shame the wise; God chose the weak things of the world to shame the strong. He chose the lowly things of this world and the despised things—and the things that are not—to nullify the things that are, so that no one may boast before him. It is because of him that you are in Christ Jesus, who has become for us wisdom from God—that is, our righteousness, holiness and redemption. Therefore, as it is written: 'Let him who boasts boast in the Lord' " (1 Cor. 1:26–31).

These verses point again to the reality of the New Testament call for servant leadership. Servants don't talk about it; they do it. As this foundational New Testament ideal unfolds, its essential quality focuses on an attitude—how we think about ourselves and about others to whom and with whom we minister.

Christian leaders appointed or elected to their posts because of their "success" must somehow humbly learn to reverse social values and respond to every situation as Christ would. And we can't build that lifestyle into people we lead unless we model it ourselves. We often want to change structures and programs; but the Holy Spirit reminds us of our *own* need for change—from pride to humility.

Trustworthiness

Life is difficult; leadership is tough. True character, particularly Christian character, enables a person to carry out a right choice in a trustworthy fashion. Anyone can say, "I will do it"; but only trustworthy people are still "doing" after forty and fifty years. Anyone can say, "I promise"; but people with integrity stake their lives on personal vows.

We live in a society that has elevated promise-breaking to a folk art. One president tells us, "I would never shred documents." Another tells us, "I never had sex with that woman." Why do the American people put up with these lies? Perhaps it's because, as someone has said, "Americans expect very little from their leaders, and they are rarely disappointed." We have collectively concluded that no candidate in any public election could possibly be serious about keeping his promises. Integrity left the political agenda years ago.

So how do we restore trustworthiness to Christian leadership? By allowing God's Spirit to produce His fruit in our lives and teaching others that same dependence. Trustworthiness may not be visible until it affects behavior. Unfortunately its absence often appears as a character flaw after disaster has already blown away the leader and all or most of his ministry as well. Lack of integrity cuts a wide swath across our lives; finances, morality, ethics, and a host of crucial leadership ingredients are all affected.

Hear again the words of Jesus to His disciples as He points their eyes to the secular politicians: "You are not to be like that" (Luke 22:26). Leadership in the church is to be different from leadership in the world. The people we encourage to assume greater ministry leadership must see trustworthiness in us, and they must know that we trust them and expect them to function with integrity.

Righteousness

In a world of highly publicized sin, Christian leaders must major in purity. The psalmist asked, "How can a young man keep his way pure? By living according to your word. I seek you with all my heart; do not let me stray from your commands. I have hidden your word in my heart that I might not sin against you" (Ps. 119:9–11). These verses point up the importance of God's Word. In fact, Psalm 119 used nine different Hebrew words to refer to God's Word.

Spiritual reality must be a day-by-day experience for church leaders. As we hold others accountable, we must ask them to hold us accountable. As we ask others to consider their spiritual status, we must stay sensitive to His work in our lives. As we ask people to consider taking more ministry responsibility, we must simplify our own lives to avoid the clutter and confusion that leadership so often requires of us.

The Bible suggests clear priorities in walking with Christ: (a) a personal relationship with Him; (b) a strong commitment to our families; and (c) a significant role in the body of Christ. When these priorities have been satisfied, we have opportunity not only to advance our own ministries but also to advance the ministries of many others by letting go of power and authority and giving it to them.

GENUINE EMPOWERMENT

The latest "buzzword" in secular leadership is *community*, which emphasizes the interrelationships in an organization, particularly among volunteers. Gifford Pinchot puts it this way: "If people feel part of the corporate community, if they feel safe and cared for, if they are passionate about the mission and values and believe that others are living by them, they will generally give good service to the whole. And if they are dedicated members of the community, it will be safe to trust them to create their own leadership roles across the organizational boundaries. As community members, they will worry less about defending their turf, trusting that if they take care of the organization, it will take care of them."[7]

Certainly no organization on earth should model Pinchot's suggestion better than the church. Yet with our bureaucratic patterns, frequent quarrels, and common autocratic leadership, we fall short of this model. What is involved in redesigning the "atmosphere" of a congregation or of any Christian ministry organization?

Understand Volunteers

Despite our culture's seemingly endless appetite for sex and violence, despite the chaotic atmosphere of a stock-market driven society, Americans are heavily involved as volunteers. Richard Kauffman reports, "Ninety-three million Americans volunteered 20.3 billion hours in 1995. This averages out to 218 hours per volunteer or 77 hours per American."[8] Almost every congregation I know literally exists on the shoulders of volunteers. Even megachurches with large pastoral staffs rely on many volunteers to do much of the hands-on work. And nobody should have greater motivation for volunteering than people in a ministry organization. Serving Christ should certainly outpace advancing a political cause or even helping society with one or more or its many ills.

When a major corporation gives workers time off because the bloodmobile is parked in the parking lot, it might be community service, but it might also be public relations. But serving one's fellow Christians because God's love compels us should make us willing to give whatever is necessary without reward. Kauffman calls us to set some priorities in volunteerism. *"Christian volunteerism should be directed toward the deepest hurts and needs.* Volunteering for youth sports, service clubs, and school projects are all constructive, social contexts for fellowship and community improvement. But specifically Christian volunteerism will be motivated by the compassion of God toward the world's deepest needs. When John the Baptist's disciples asked whether he was the Messiah, Jesus replied: 'The blind receive sight, the lame walk, those who have leprosy are cured, the deaf hear, the dead are raised, and the good news is preached to the poor' (Matt. 11:5, NIV). One sign that the Messiah had come was that God in Christ was ministering to the least and lowest on the earth."[9]

Also don't try to force volunteers to get excited about things *you* want done. Motivation rests in unleashing *their* interests and heartfelt concerns, not imposing the church's agenda. Christians released and empowered to follow through on their own gifts and calling from God respond at high levels of commitment and competence.

Reject Micromanaging

We discussed this earlier, but it deserves emphasizing again if we are to learn to "let go." Are you a micromanager? Take the following quiz to find out.

- Do you set goals and tell your staff how to accomplish them?
- Do you require specific hours and times for people to be "on the job" and get irritated when they're not there?
- Do you take it personally when a volunteer lets you down by not following through on an assignment?
- Do you sound patronizing when you work with volunteers?

- Do you (consciously or subconsciously) encourage people to fit a leadership pattern that looks like you?
- Are you curt or rude to people who continuously ask why things are done a certain way or why they are done at all?
- Do volunteers in your organization continuously come to you to ask how they should do things?
- Do your meetings drag on to the point that people lose interest in coming?
- Do you feel threatened or envious when team members succeed beyond your expectations?
- Do you take yourself or your position too seriously?

If you answered yes to more than five of these questions, you need to think seriously about letting go of close-up managing.

Facilitate Involvement

Team leadership is an applied science and a useful art. We release people to serve by believing they are capable of using their freedom to enhance the ministry. Rather than thinking of meetings as a necessary evil, we value the act of convening as a primary part of our leadership roles, and we design those meetings for group decision-making rather than as a platform for our own speeches.

Peter Block talks about "the end of leadership" and describes his experience in organizational renewal. Revitalization, he says, commonly begins somewhere in the middle of an organization, not at the top. He disdains management which denies that motivation and responsibility can exist without the blessing of those in charge. "We will always need clear structures, measures, and rules to live by. The workplace begins to change only when employees join together in choosing the structure, measures, and rules. Clinging to our attraction to leadership keeps change in the hands of the few. We need to transfer it to the many. This is the power of citizenship. The task of the boss, then, is to convene people and engage them in the everyday challenges of how to plan, organize, discipline, and insure that the right people are on the team and doing the job right. Bosses become conveners and clarifiers, not visionaries, role models, or motivators."[10]

Delegation is the old word; the word commonly used today is *empowerment*. This means learning to let go—of authority, finances, decision-making, control—and "decentralizing" ourselves in order to advance and enhance the ministry of others.

The ideas in this chapter, like many others in this book, differ from traditional managerial practices. But secular management at its peak of research success at the beginning of the twenty-first century has in many ways returned to a biblical format. Call it participatory leadership, team leadership, or servant leadership—it is precisely what Jesus taught the disciples and what He expected them to produce in the early church. Now people like Stephen Covey and Peter Drucker say similar things in different words.

Perhaps for the first time in the history of management science the major secular spokesmen are lining up with what the Bible has commanded for two thousand years. C. William Pollard addresses the issue of empowerment in an interesting way. "Will the leader please stand up? Not the president, or the person with the most distinguished title, but the role model. Not the highest-paid person in the group, but the risk-taker. Not the person with the largest car or the biggest home, but the servant. Not the person who promotes himself or herself, but the promoter of others. Not the administrator, but the initiator. Not the taker, but the giver. Not the talker, but the listener."[11]

CHAPTER 11
Designing a Climate-Controlled Gymnasium:
Leadership Atmosphere

WHILE RIDING MY BIKE one day, I passed a small panel van with the lettering "Johnson Controls" on the side. This company services large business complexes and educational institutions by installing and operating equipment that regulates the air-conditioning and heating units in each of the buildings. The intent, of course, is to achieve the ideal interior "climate" for employees to function at the highest level. In a symbolic sense that is exactly what good leaders do—they create a climate, an environment, in which other people feel comfortable serving the Lord. This chapter examines three components that contribute to positive "climate control," but first we pause for a look at one of the original protectors of spiritual environment.

BIBLICAL BACKGROUND: BARNABAS

Every time Barnabas is mentioned in the New Testament, he is seen offering a positive model of collegiality. He was a man of faith, and one of the earliest demonstrations of that faith appears in Acts 4:34–37.

Faith in the Church

Barnabas believed in the church so much that he gave what he had and joined the ministry at Jerusalem. His given name was Joseph, and he was nicknamed "Barnabas" ("Son of Encouragement") after his brothers and sisters at Jerusalem watched him in action with other believers.

I've always been impressed that Barnabas stayed a faithful member of the church without branching out on his own. He certainly had the opportunity to form an attractive splinter group and even had a ready-made name—"The Sons of Consolation." But Barnabas was a churchman of the first line, an early Christian who understood the difference between stewardship and ownership in the service of the heavenly King.

Faith in People

Barnabas also had faith in people. Shortly after Saul's conversion Barnabas introduced him to the Jerusalem church. "When he came to Jerusalem, he tried to join the disciples, but they were all afraid of him, not believing that he really was a disciple. But Barnabas took him and brought him to the apostles. He told them how Saul on his journey had seen the Lord and that the Lord had spoken to him, and how in Damascus he had preached fearlessly in the name of Jesus" (Acts 9:26–27).

We find it difficult to think that a church might not want the apostle Paul as a member, but of course, he was not an apostle at that time; he was the feared persecutor from Tarsus. Yet Barnabas believed God had changed Saul's life, and so the reaction in Jerusalem could have been expressed this way: "Any friend of Barnabas is a friend of ours."

This display of faith in people faced some major tests, as we learn toward the end of Acts 15. Barnabas and Paul "had such a sharp disagreement that they parted company. Barnabas took Mark and sailed for Cyprus, but Paul chose Silas and left, commended by the brothers to the grace of the Lord" (15:39–40).

Let's not minimize this argument. Paul deemed Mark irresponsible and immature on the first missionary journey and was not willing to take him a second time. But Barnabas had faith in Mark's future ministry and returned with him to Cyprus to enter a period of personal discipleship for the young man. After public ministry at Antioch, Barnabas settled into personal mentoring with John Mark. God used him to develop one of the outstanding young leaders of the church whom Paul later sent to Colosse (Col. 4:10). Paul said Mark was effective in ministry (2 Tim. 4:11), and of course later the Spirit of God used Mark to author the second Gospel.

Faith in Himself

Perhaps of greatest interest to us in this book, however, is that Barnabas had faith in himself. He demonstrated this clearly at Antioch when, having been placed in charge of the work there, he showed no selfish pride, no insecurity or defensiveness in that leadership role. Barnabas knew Saul's brilliance better than anyone in the early church. He doubtless understood that Saul could "out-preach" and "out-teach" him week in and week out. But Barnabas had designed a climate in which he would comfortably work with the brilliant young rabbi, making room for their different styles of leadership in the same congregation.

In a real sense Barnabas incarnates team leadership. He was willing to take whatever ministry God sent to him, whether public or private, he served with compassion, and he designed a ministry climate in which different personalities could thrive.

AN ATTRACTIVE PLACE TO WORK

I recall reading in *Time* magazine some years ago that the average American living to seventy years of age spends twenty years sleeping, twenty years working, six years eating, seven years playing, five years dressing, one year on the telephone, three years waiting for others, five months tying shoes, and the rest for everything else, including one and a half years in church. I can't document those numbers, but if they are even close, I would think a comfortable bed and a pleasant atmosphere at work would be high on everyone's priority list. Experts have observed that though salary and benefits remain the primary concerns, less obvious but very important factors have emerged with amazing impact.

Informality

Interesting, isn't it, that a quest for a relaxed and casual atmosphere follows right on the heels of salary and benefits? People shudder under our current stressful society, and when they see leaders making an effort to reduce the pressure, whether in full-time staff or volunteer ministries, they respond in positive ways.

Collegiality

Barnabas was ahead of his time in providing a friendly, nonthreatening atmosphere for spiritual growth and ministry. Most people (there are exceptions) want to avoid politics and infighting in ministry roles, and a spirit of mutual love takes collegiality a significant step higher in a church or Christian organization. Hebrews 13 begins with a clear-cut command: "Keep on loving each other as brothers." The New Testament frequently commands us to serve each other in a spirit of love; the very next verse tells us to spread the love externally through the practice of hospitality: "Do not forget to entertain strangers, for by so doing some people have entertained angels without knowing it" (13:2).

The writer moved from mentioning the love of brothers to mentioning the love of strangers. Elders, deacons, Sunday school teachers, ushers, choir members, and volunteers of all kinds can grow in that kind of environment. The writer of Hebrews also wrote, "Remember your leaders, who spoke the word of God to you. Consider the outcome of their way of life and imitate their faith. Jesus Christ is the same yesterday and today and forever" (13:7–8). The Bible spells out definite requirements for elders and deacons (see chapter 12) and implies numerous qualifications for congregational teachers.

We must not only *select our leaders carefully;* we must also *follow our leaders faithfully.* The Bible points to leaders as models, and though Hebrews 13:7 may refer specifically to martyrs, we may surely draw a generalization. Following our spiritual leaders does not include criticizing and complaining, common habits among too many Christians.

Perhaps most important in this context of love both inside and outside the church is the reminder that we should *encourage our leaders regularly*. We achieve climate control by both word and behavior. The writer of Hebrews has said earlier in this epistle, "Let us consider how we may spur one another on toward love and good deeds. . . . [and] let us encourage one another—and all the more as you see the Day approaching" (10:24–25).

Fairness

Workplaces that are pleasant and attractive are noted for impartiality and equity. In today's society that means equal pay for equal work. And in a volunteer ministry, fairness means consistency in policy, a reasonable amount of responsibility, and genuine recognition for performance. At risk here is not just recruitment, but retention. People respond to and stay with ministries in which they perceive a genuine fairness in issues they consider important.

Nurture

Christian organizations, particularly congregations, ought to be primary examples of learning-while-serving. As a church continuously renews its members in spiritual vitality, it continually renews itself. Max De Pree puts it this way: "Vital organizations have adopted an attitude of life-time learning, and they help their members make everyday learning a reality in their lives. The nourishment of individuals lies at the heart of vitality in organizations, and the nourishment of individuals begins with the opportunity to learn."[1]

Focus

Perhaps I'm reflecting personal taste here, but my Swiss blood abhors anything that is disheveled or disorganized—rooms, meetings, clothing, desks, and work environment. Professionals respond by organizing the disorganized and "sheveling" the disheveled. Volunteers, however, tend to react to disorder by declining to become involved or leaving when they sense leaders lack purpose and focus. The answer is a solid grasp on the mission. The ministry opportunities we offer, and to which we expect people to respond positively, must arise from the mission. To quote De Pree again, "The best non-profit groups begin with truth and end with fidelity to their missions."[2]

Consistency

In a way this last component layers the first five. People aren't looking for *occasional* informality, collegiality, fairness, nurture focus, and certainly not *occasional* allegiance to the mission. Consistency in leadership means that people know what they can expect from us and we follow through in precisely that manner. Leading by surprise is manipulation, not motivation. I have known a number of pastors who have stayed with effective ministries for several decades. They represent a variety of preaching styles, personalities, and approaches to congregational life. But in every case one finds a consistency in leadership.

A DISTINCT PHILOSOPHY OF MINISTRY

The philosophy of postmodernity has dethroned revelation, tradition, and even reason; all the familiar players are off the stage, and the acceptance of any opinion on any subject is the politically correct view of modern times. Yet tradition is never a sure guard against doctrinal failure, and church size is no guarantee of spiritual quality. If we face the future with total dependence on the sovereignty of God and the power of His Word, if our focus remains exclusively biblical in everything we do, then we will avoid marrying the spirit of this age and becoming a widow in the next.

Stability in times of chaos requires a clear and biblical philosophy of ministry. Philosophy of ministry simply describes how we go about fulfilling our mission based on what we believe and practice as an organization. The following series of contrasts points up essential elements in cultivating a meaningful atmosphere or "climate" for our workers.

Effectiveness, Not Success

In their book *No Little Places* Ron Klassen and John Koessler talk about "five myths of ministry success." They are worth reproducing here.

1. The numbers myth: To be significant, a ministry must be big.
2. The big-place myth: To be significant, a ministry must be in a big place.
3. The recognition myth: One measure of the significance of one's ministry is how much recognition he receives for it.
4. The career myth: Career advances are signs of a significant ministry.
5. The cure-for-inferiority myth: If a leader can succeed professionally, he'll no longer feel inferior.[3]

When I saw this little paperback begin in such a manner, I knew I had found a book close to my own heart in philosophy of ministry. No one wants a gravel-road church in an interstate world, but at no point do the Scriptures give us any basis for justifying spiritual health on the basis of size. True, in the early chapters of Acts we read of some large numbers of people coming to Christ. Then all of a sudden those numbers fade, and Luke never mentioned the size of any congregation on Paul's three missionary journeys, nor do we have any idea of the size of any of the congregations to which the New Testament epistles were written.

Ministry effectiveness begins with a Christ-centered, Bible-focused congregation determined to be in their personal, family, and corporate life precisely what God wants of them, and it makes no difference whether they number fifteen, fifteen hundred, or fifteen thousand.

But the success/effectiveness contrast addresses more than quantity. The best resources in secular leadership today tend to debunk the effectiveness of success and highlight the learning value of *failure*. Rapidly growing churches and high-profit organizations face some of the same problems. David and Mark Nadler address this issue. "The good news is that self-destructive attitudes such as arrogance, insularity, and complacency don't assume their full form overnight. The bad news is that they can slowly creep up on an organization, becoming deeply entrenched before anyone is really aware of the change that has taken place. Astute leaders need to pay attention to their symptoms and root out those attitudes and practices when they appear."[4]

Success is easily measured in our world by numbers and popularity. *Effectiveness*, on the other hand, cuts right to the heart of our ministry— a clear-cut mission, achievable goals, carefully selected priorities, and an evaluation of ministry performance.

Unity, Not Quarrelling

When I began my doctoral study many years ago, I interviewed at two institutions, one of which was the University of Kansas. When I visited with the graduate dean in the school of education at that school, we had a fascinating conversation that went something like this:

"Did you say you are an administrator at a Bible college?"

"Yes."

"Is that a church-related school of some kind?"

"Yes, certainly church-related, but not affiliated with any particular denomination."

(pause)

"I used to go to church."

"Really? Tell me about it."

"Yes, I used to go to church, and I remember one thing about my church."

"And what is that?"

"They fight."

I still find his response startling. Imagine the things he could have named—preaching, buildings, music, denominational affiliation. Yet this man chose to associate church people with quarrelling in a discussion with a person he'd known for only five or ten minutes.

In my opinion, *working at unity in the congregation stands right beside proclaiming the gospel as two major priorities of ministry.* Many congregations could experience revival in a few weeks without an increased budget, extra meetings, or even a tent. They need only put into practice the crystal-clear words Paul wrote to the church at Philippi: Be "like-minded, having the same love, being one in spirit and purpose. Do nothing out of selfish ambition or vain conceit, but in humility consider others better than yourselves. Each of you should look not only to your own interests, but also to the interests of others. Your attitude should be the same as that of Christ Jesus" (Phil. 2:2–5).

According to these verses the key to an effective philosophy of ministry is unity among believers. The word "if," which appears four times in verse 1, could be translated "since." In other words, we *do* have spiritual unity with Christ; we *do* have comfort from His love; we *do* have fellowship with His spirit; and we *do* have tenderness and compassion. These are the basis of "being one in spirit and purpose." An effective ministry does not begin with programs or committees; it begins with attitude: "Each of you should look not only to your own interests, but also to the interests of others."

Visionary, Not Nostalgic

Some churches, and even entire denominations, still follow the practice of expecting associate staff members to resign when a senior pastor leaves. They apparently assume that these people are of lesser importance and therefore should be replaced if the senior pastor so wishes. Even though a similar practice happens in secular corporations, it is hardly held up in leadership literature as a desirable practice. In terms of biblical guidelines, I find it reprehensible. Associate staff should be called to the church, not to the coattails of an outgoing pastor.

Whenever practice of the past gets in the way of performance in the present, vision has been swallowed up by nostalgia *and we find ourselves once again doing something just because "we've always done it this way."*

Biblical, Not Cultural

Though the gospel has always been transcultural, Christians have frequently been tempted to adapt so dramatically to their cultural surroundings that they fade into the scenery of the world and cannot even be seen. To be sure, this is most often done from sincere motives, a desire to contextualize the gospel or to be "relevant to the times." Commonly seen in the Renaissance and again in the Enlightenment, such behavior marks much of evangelicalism today. We are hooked on futurism, movements, groups, and slogans.

The shaky theology of some church-growth leaders has influenced many by its pragmatic outcome-centered approach—if it works, it must be right. John MacArthur warns, "The contemporary church's abandonment of *sola Scriptura* as the regulative principle has opened the church to some of the grossest imaginable abuses—including honky-tonk church services, a carnival sideshow atmosphere, and wrestling exhibitions. Even the broadest, most liberal application of the regulative principle would have a corrective effect on such abuses."[5]

Healthy churches must be based on theological rather than sociological foundations. Herein rests my primary problem with much contemporary theology and much of what we let pass for Christian leadership. Too many have taken their cues from sociological pragmatism (as suggested earlier), ignoring the true dynamic of biblical theology, and even failing to evaluate cultural and sociological insights by the measure of Scripture. Os Guinness picks up this point in his critique of the church-growth movement. "On the one hand, its theological understanding is often superficial, with almost no element of biblical criticism. As a well-known proponent states, 'I don't deal with theology, I'm simply a methodologist'—as if his theology were thereby guaranteed to remain critical and his methodology neutral. But in fact, theology is rarely more than marginal in the church growth movement and discussion of the traditional marks of the church is virtually nonexistent. Instead, methodology, or technique, is at the center and in control. The result is a methodology only occasionally in search of a theology."[6]

Rather than programs and paradigms, first-century believers were marked by unity and generosity. "All the believers were one in heart and mind. No one claimed that any of his possessions was his own, but they shared everything they had. With great power the apostles continued to testify to the resurrection of the Lord Jesus, and much grace was upon them all. There were no needy persons among them. For from time to time those who owned lands or houses sold them, brought the money from the sales and put it at the apostles' feet, and it was distributed to anyone as he had need" (Acts 4:32–35).

No wonder the world was interested! The believers spoke the Word of God boldly and proclaimed the name of Jesus and the resurrection—*wherever they went.* And their message carried meaning because people knew what kind of relationships they maintained when they were together. Raymond Ortlund reminds us, "The Epistles command believers to unite together on the basis of their new family relationship in Christ. Over and over come the instructions: Suffer together (1 Cor. 12:26), rejoice together (Rom. 12:15), carry each other's burdens (Gal. 6:2), restore each other (6:1), pray for each other (Rom. 15:30), teach and admonish each other (Col. 3:16), refresh each other (Rom. 15:32), encourage each other (1:12), forgive each other (Eph. 4:32), confess to each other (James 5:16), be truthful with each other (Eph. 4:25), spur each other to good deeds (Heb. 10:24), and give to each other (Phil. 4:14–15)."[7]

Most New Testament students agree that Ephesians identifies biblical goals for the church and describes how they can be achieved. In that letter Paul dealt with neither error nor heresy. Instead he sought to expand the spiritual horizons of his readers, particularly in relationship to the body of Christ. But where in Ephesians do we find mention of programs and statistics? Where in Ephesians did Paul talk about growth or plateauing? Where is there any reference to buildings and fund drives, both of which are believed today to be marks of a "healthy church"?

Of course, we find none of those elements. Instead, the apostle described humble people making spiritual progress with God and each other, and offered a formula that could change a church of any size from sickness to health in a matter of weeks: "Be completely humble and gentle; be patient, bearing with one another in love. Make every effort to keep the unity of the Spirit through the bond of peace. There is one body and one Spirit—just as you were called to one hope when you were called—one Lord, one faith, one baptism; one God and Father of all, who is over all and through all and in all" (Eph. 4:2–6).

A distinct philosophy of ministry which follows these guidelines will first target God's priorities and then allow Him to produce in our churches what He wants—from the inside out. Yes, God wants to do a new thing in this world and through His church by His power. But let's make sure the methods, movements, and manipulations of modern cultural Christianity don't get in the way.

A MINISTRY ON THE MOVE

Stephen Covey's book *The Seven Habits of Highly Successful People* was a bestseller for years, and more recently he has written *The Seven Habits of a Successful Organization.* In a recent article in *Leader to Leader,* Covey changed his adjective "successful" to "effective," referring there to "the habits of effective organizations."[8]

Covey claims that successful (effective) organizations fluidly move in a positive posture toward improvement. And he starts with a basic premise: "Organizational behavior is the collective outcome of individual behavior." As we design a climate for ministry, as we identify the right people for the right places, our ministry organizations should also move in a manner similar to the way Covey describes corporations.

From Control to Commitment

The climate in which people serve should not be dominated by one person or a small group of leaders. Covey reviews this important point. "I had an opportunity to interview the leaders of several Malcolm Baldridge-Award-Winning organizations, and I asked each, 'What was the toughest struggle you had?' To a person, they all said, 'Giving up control.' They all feared the consequences of letting go. But ultimately they found their fears were groundless—they found an imagined resource capability that emerged when there was a common vision and a common value system."[9]

One can imagine that a group of new recruits heading into battle might require the control of an experienced sergeant or well-trained lieutenant. But a congregation or ministry organization certainly represents a completely different culture with very different needs. If any unit of society needs to move from a culture of control to a culture of commitment, it is surely the church of Jesus Christ.

From Secrecy to Information

Obviously church leaders must guard confidential matters, but the negative communication patterns in many churches tend to be more crippled by unnecessary secrecy than an overabundance of information.

From Labor to Learning

In 1998 the U.S. Bureau of Labor Statistics Report indicated that up to 70 percent of workplace learning is informal. Yet U.S. businesses annually spend "millions of staff hours and nearly $60 billion on training."[10] The contrast Covey addresses means that we no longer talk about the work people do (labor) but how they develop and grow in the nurturing climate which we have designed (learning). It may be worth keeping in mind that secular business, so concerned with creating learning organizations, has come to believe that successful business measured in profits requires consistent learning. How much more should the church with its emphasis on Bible knowledge and understanding see itself not so much as an organization in which people *work* but as one in which they *learn*.

From Fear to Faith

Can you imagine someone afraid of his or her pastor? Can you imagine a volunteer afraid to show up at church because of a tongue-lashing received last week? Can you imagine a congregation fearing what a group of elders might decide in secretive closed sessions? For many people this reflects not imagination but reality. A climate conducive to learning and serving begins with leaders who inspire trust and faith rather than fear.

From Competition to Cooperation

The athletic metaphor in our society has driven us to design almost everything around "the competitive edge." Television commercials commonly remind us how much a certain product out-performs its "competitors." We buy cars that look newer and drive faster than those of the neighbors, and winning contests becomes a major activity of many congregations striving for "church of the year" honors or recognition as the fastest-growing church in a district or state.

The Bible calls us to work together, to stand side by side and bear one another's burdens. Paul liked to use athletic metaphors based on the Greco-Roman world in which he lived, a culture not unlike our own. And in Matthew 11:29 Jesus talked about the yoke, an instrument of mutuality and cooperation.

From Past to Future

Here Covey means focus, and he deals with what we have already de-scribed above in the nostalgia/vision section of this chapter. Effective congregations recognize God's hand in the past and express gratitude. But they also wonder what new vistas may open up in the weeks, months, and years ahead.

From Market to Mission

Effective organizations should be moving from an emphasis on market to an emphasis on mission. Our society's fascination with the state of the economy can easily draw us away from a determination to fulfill what God wants from us. Philosophy of ministry begins with a simply stated yet easily misunderstood question: "Why has God raised up this church in this place, at this time, and what does He want from us?"

All of us in leadership roles become spiritual meteorologists, describ-ing the favorable climate available to those who would serve. But though meteorologists tell what happened in the past and what we might expect in the future, they don't *design* the climate. That is what leaders do to elevate and activate the ministries God has given us.

CHAPTER 12
Designated Hitters at Bat: Church Officers

THE NUMBER-ONE SPORTS STORY for 1998 was not Michael Jordan's involvement in the Bulls' three-time championship but the home-run crown chase between Mark McGwire and Sammy Sosa. Baseball, called America's national pastime, needed a shot of adrenaline, which McGwire provided with seventy home runs, trailed by Sosa's sixty-six. Both players played regularly on defense as well, but even without the American league rules operating for them in every game, they were without doubt "designated hitters."

Every church leadership team contains designated hitters. Some are pastors, and others are elders or deacons. Some denominations choose not to use those terms, while others add several other titles. But in the pages of the New Testament, only two emerge, and the detail with which the Scriptures treat them reminds us of their importance.

BIBLICAL BACKGROUND: PAUL

The elders of the church at Ephesus went down to visit Paul at Miletus, about thirty miles away. They sensed that this was no ordinary meeting. Sensing that greater difficulties awaited him in Jerusalem, Paul reminded the elders that they should carry on the work at Ephesus, which he had faithfully taught them to do.

Servant of the Lord

"From Miletus, Paul sent to Ephesus for the elders of the church. When they arrived, he said to them: 'You know how I lived the whole time I was with you, from the first day I came into the province of Asia. I served the Lord with great humility and with tears, although I was severely tested by the plots of the Jews. You know that I have not hesitated to preach anything that would be helpful to you but have taught you publicly and from house to house. I have declared to both Jews and Greeks that they must turn to God in repentance and have faith in our Lord Jesus' " (Acts 20:17–21).

Here Paul referred almost exclusively to himself, indicating the kind of ministry he had at Ephesus. What does an effective leader do with his team? One of the answers is in verse 20.

Team leaders are teaching leaders. They take time to explain the issues involved—so that other people can be more productive by utilizing what they have learned. Paul's remarks center on his faithful service to Jesus Christ.

Servant of the Word

Paul had spent three years in Ephesus, declaring to the elders there "the whole will of God" (20:27); his ministry was Word-centered. Once people put their trust in Christ and become God's children through His grace, they need building up in spiritual matters, including an emphasis on holy living and godliness. He did not manipulate the congregation by the power of his own personality, but rather he taught them skillfully and carefully from the Word of God, a balanced ministry that emphasized both evangelism ("they must turn to God," 20:21) and edification (he taught them "publicly and from house to house," 20:20). Only God's Word of grace can build up believers (20:32).

Believers also need training for their ministries. And Paul did that with the Ephesian elders; he urged them to "be shepherds of the church of God" (20:28).

Servant of Others

Paul then said to the elders, "In everything I did, I showed you that by this kind of hard work we must help the weak, remembering the words the Lord Jesus himself said: 'It is more blessed to give than to receive' " (20:35).

Now Paul focused on the responsibility of the Ephesian elders. What *he* had done in the past, *they* should do now. This means they would need to guard themselves (20:28) as well as all the flock of believers. As Jesus was a Shepherd, so they were to be shepherds—overseers of the work at Ephesus.

The danger came not only from external infiltration ("savage wolves will come in among you," 20:29), but also from internal perversion ("Even from your own number men will arise and distort the truth," 20:30). By warning the elders that these things were impending, he hoped to help them ward off the attacks of Satan.

When Paul left them, they knew they would never see him again (20:36–38). This was an emotional time—not unlike the experience of any leader leaving a church or ministry for the last time. But the crucial part of the passage does not center in sadness over Paul's departure. Instead Paul's main concern was that they carry on the ministry faithfully ("be shepherds ... I commit you to God," 20:28, 32). Leadership must go on even though a leader leaves. As seen in Paul's relationships with Barnabas, Silas, Luke, Timothy, Epaphroditus, and the Ephesians elders, this amazing apostle was always concerned with transferring the mantle of leadership to others.

SELECTING THE ELDERS

An old familiar saying reminds us that "accidents will happen." But we can't afford an accident when we call a pastor or elect officers in a church. The axiom seems clear—the more care we take at the outset in selecting church leaders, the less grief we will experience later. The qualifications found in 1 Timothy 3:2–7 apply equally to pastors and elders. Four times in these verses Paul used the word *must* to emphasize how imperative it is that we select only qualified leaders for key positions in a congregation.

High standards for leadership help provide a deterrent to doctrinal failings and the selection of unworthy candidates. Those same high standards would also provide a challenge to worthy candidates. The following steps are called for in choosing leaders God's way.

Examine Their Calling

"Here is a trustworthy saying: If anyone sets his heart on being an overseer, he desires a noble task" (1 Tim. 3:1).

There is always some kind of "call" involved in serving the Lord, not just for pastors but for lay leaders as well. Elders, deacons, teachers—there should be a sense of vocation for all ministry roles, and certainly for the office of elder. Wanting to be an elder is commendable because God places a premium on committed leadership. In Old Testament times, leaders were anointed, and today they are appointed or elected, no less a distinction of responsibility.

Episkopos, the Greek term for overseer, appears five times in the New Testament.

> "Paul and Timothy, servants of Christ Jesus, To all the saints in Christ Jesus at Philippi, together with the overseers *[episkopoi]* and deacons" (Phil. 1:1).

> "Here is a trustworthy saying: If anyone sets his heart on being an overseer *[episkopos]*, he desires a noble task. Now the overseer *[episkopos]* must be above reproach, the husband of but one wife, temperate, self-controlled, respectable, hospitable, able to teach, not given to drunkenness, not violent but gentle, not quarrelsome, not a lover of money" (1 Tim. 3:1–3).

> "Since an overseer *[episkopos]* is entrusted with God's work, he must be blameless—not overbearing, not quick-tempered, not given to drunkenness, not violent, not pursuing dishonest gain" (Titus 1:7).

> "For you were like sheep going astray, but now you have returned to the Shepherd and Overseer *[episkopos]* of your souls" (1 Pet. 2:25).

Episkopos seems to refer to the same office suggested by *prebyteros,* often translated "elder" as well (Acts 20:17). In Greek culture the word was used of officials presiding over a civil or religious organization; in the context of 1 Timothy it refers to a local congregation. The last word in 1 Timothy 3:1 is *ergon,* which means "work" ("task," NIV). Before Paul identified the qualifications of elders, he wanted Timothy and others to understand that ministry means work and that people appointed to the office of elder should expect just that. "Churches, organizations, and the communities they serve . . . need leaders who know how God has made and gifted them for service and to willingly serve Christ and those placed in their care. These groups need leaders who have skills to equip others and to 'team with them' in ministry. We need leaders who will step down from the head table and serve in the kitchen. Ministries and organizations will survive in the twenty-first century when men and women stop following self-conceived concepts of leadership and adopt Jesus' teachings and examples."[1]

Examine Their Qualifications

"Now the overseer must be above reproach, the husband of but one wife, temperate, self-controlled, respectable, hospitable, able to teach, not given to drunkenness, not violent but gentle, not quarrelsome, not a lover of money" (1 Tim. 3:2–3).

Above reproach. This phrase means that an elder must be one against whom others can bring no legitimate charge of wrongdoing. Since this item appears first, it might even refer to accusations related to the other fourteen qualifications in verses 2–7.

Husband of one wife. Does this phrase mean elders must be men? Does it mean an elder can have only one wife at a time? Does it mean he can never have been divorced? Does it mean that elders must be married and that single men cannot serve? Literally, the verse says that an elder must be "a one-woman man." Perhaps instead of worrying about whom this qualification excludes, we should emphasize its positive side, which tells us that elders must be devoted to their wives. Adulterous and divorced elders present a contemporary issue in the church. However, more frequently we see elder candidates who would not be disqualified by any of these external issues yet whose behavior at home does not meet biblical standards.

Temperate. This word *(nēphalios),* which is used only here and in 3:11 and Titus 2:2, means to be sober, or serious and dignified.

Self-controlled. This word, which translates *sōphrona,* appears only here and in Titus 1:8 and 2:5. The term carries the sense of conducting oneself with restraint, particularly in public.

Respectable. This word, which translates *kosmion,* has to do with orderliness and design, but the ideas of honor and respectability certainly fit as well. In 1 Timothy 2:9 the New International Version translates this word as "modesty" in reference to godly women.

Hospitable. The word *philoxenon* reminds us that elders should love strangers. Hospitality is an important Christian virtue in any era.

Able to teach. This phrase is used only here and in 2 Timothy 2:24, "And the Lord's servant must not quarrel; instead, he must be kind to everyone, able to teach, not resentful." Elders need more than just knowledge of the Scriptures; they must also be able to communicate God's Word to others.

Not given to much wine. The four words "given to much wine" come from one Greek word that means "beside wine." Aristotle used the word to describe people exhibiting drunken behavior.

Not violent. This qualification speaks for itself. How ugly a thought to imagine elders almost coming to blows in a business meeting.

Gentle. Instead of violent or drunken, elders are to be gracious, kindly, considerate, magnanimous, and meek.

Not quarrelsome. The American military talks about "noncombatants." That word should always describe elders, but Paul's word also includes being noncontentious.

Not a lover of money. This translates one Greek word which appears only here in the New Testament. This speaks to the question of motivation and would certainly disqualify many who claim to serve Christ in the wide media arenas of our day.

These standards emphasize the person's *spiritual* condition. They help answer the question, Is the potential elder qualified spiritually to serve in a spiritual capacity.[2] Every adjective used in this list is masculine. The term "overseer" is masculine as well. These observations (coupled with the phrase "husband of one wife") suggest that only men are to be church elders.

Examine Their Families

"He must manage his own family well and see that his children obey him with proper respect. (If anyone does not know how to manage his own family, how can he take care of God's church?)" (1 Tim. 3:4–5).

People who would be leaders in the church must first demonstrate leadership at home. An elder's children must be obedient and respectful in public as well as at home. Don't miss the impact of the rhetorical question in verse 5; one who can't manage properly at home should not be asked to manage in the church. Deficiency in leadership at home disqualifies one from serving in leadership at church.

Examine Their Maturity

"He must not be a recent convert, or he may become conceited and fall under the same judgment as the devil" (3:6).

In this verse we find another qualification—not a recent convert. The Greek word *neophytos,* which appears only here in the New Testament, literally means "newly planted." From it we get the word *neophyte.* No newcomer should be rushed into church leadership.

The words "become conceited" translate the verb *typhoō,* "to wrap in smoke, to puff up . . . to be clouded with pride."[3] This suggests that neophytes stand in constant danger of allowing pride to get into their hearts, much in the same way smoke from a fire gets in one's eyes.

Examine Their Reputations

"He must also have a good reputation with outsiders, so that he will not fall into disgrace and into the devil's trap" (3:7).

Church leaders must have a reputation of integrity with the world, with those in the church whom they would lead, and with God Himself.

What does Paul have in mind here? Obviously, no church wants elders who have a reputation for open anger, bad language, and regular drinking at the local bar. But surely other matters are important too. What about rudeness? How about bad debts of even a small amount? Should a man be an elder if he allows his property to deteriorate so badly it becomes an eyesore in his neighborhood? These things make up public reputation among unbelievers, and we dare not take them lightly. The phrase, "the devil's trap," refers to either that which trapped the devil (pride) or what the devil uses to trap immature leaders (also pride). Most commentators believe that the cause of Satan's fall from the status of archangel to chief demon centered in pride; therefore proud people are subject to the same judgment as the devil.

SCORING THE DEACONS

The word *deacon* comes from *diakonos* and *diakonia,* two important New Testament terms, each occuring more than two dozen times. The first means "minister" or "servant," and the second means either "servant" or "service." One good example appears in Colossians. "You learned it from Epaphras, our dear fellow servant, who is a faithful minister of Christ on our behalf. . . . This is the gospel that you heard and that has been proclaimed to every creature under heaven, and of which I, Paul, have become a servant. . . . I have become its servant by the commission God gave me to present to you the word of God in its fullness" (Col. 1:7, 23, 25).

In 1 Timothy 3:8–10, 12 Paul linked deacons with elders (3:1–7), showing that deacons represent a second office in the church.

When a congregation considers the election or appointment of deacons, it needs to examine their qualifications in four areas.

Examine Their Credibility

"Deacons, likewise, are to be men worthy of respect, sincere, not indulging in much wine, and not pursuing dishonest gain. They must keep hold of the deep truths of the faith with a clear conscience" (1 Tim. 3:8–9). These two verses include five qualifications for deacons. Two more are given in verse 10 and two more in verse 12, for a total of nine.

Worthy of respect. The word *semnos,* "dignified or serious," is also used of deacons' wives and older men (3:11; Titus 2:2).

146

I remember a *Peanuts* strip in which Peppermint Patty said to Linus, "I should be an evangelist. Today I convinced a kid that my religion was better than his."

Linus responds, "How did you do that?"

Peppermint Patty says, "I hit him with my lunchbox."

Deacons should not hit anyone with a lunchbox—or with anything else. They must display dignity and serious-mindedness in their ministry.

Sincere. This Greek word, *dilogos,* used only here in the New Testament, means "not two-tongued," that is, not hypocritical, not saying one thing to one person and something entirely opposite to another person.

Not indulging in much wine. This is a longer and even stronger expression than the phrase "not given to much wine," which was included in verse 3 in relation to elders.

Not pursuing dishonest gain. This phrase appears only here and in Titus 1:7. Perhaps the office of deacon holds a temptation here, since churches often ask deacons to handle money and other valuable resources. Some believe that the leaders selected in Acts 6 actually held the office of deacon, but perhaps they were serving in that capacity without holding a formal office. Nevertheless it does seem clear that right from the beginning deacons were to free up elders to give attention to prayer and Bible teaching.

Keeping the deep truths of the faith. The Greek word rendered "deep truths" is literally "mystery," which in the first century meant *truth revealed,* whereas today we think of a mystery as knowledge withheld. Deacons are to be faithful to God's Word.

Examine Their Service

"They must first be tested; and then if there is nothing against them, let them serve as deacons" (1 Tim. 3:10).

I remember years ago attending the great Bible conference meetings at the Winona Lake Conference Grounds in Indiana. My favorite soloist in those years was Bill Carle, who could sing everything from opera to spirituals. I remember well his rendition of "Let the Church Roll On."

> There's a deacon in the church
> And he don't deac right.
> Well, what are you gonna do?
> Have him up, teach him how,
> And let the church roll on.

This sounds like a good idea in many churches. Certainly it reminds us that congregations must pay careful attention to how their leaders perform in relation to biblical mandates. For deacons, service is certainly the name of the game, and as they serve they model Christian living for the entire congregation. Charles Swindoll puts it this way. "No selfless act is so small, no good deed is so insignificant, that God cannot see and approve. After all, what we do as servants is not for men's eyes. It is not for our own glory that faithful service is so clearly prescribed throughout Scripture but for the glory of God. And God has given us the incredible honor of being His stewards to carry out the work of Jesus Christ through faithful service—in our neighborhoods and around the world."[4]

Verse 10 calls for two more qualifications for deacons: They must be tested, and they must be irreproachable. Presumably, testing serves the purpose of discovering that they are without reproach. Such evaluation actually takes place in three stages: the test, the proof by testing, and the approval as a result of testing. In other words, we should not elect or appoint men as deacons whose lives have not been examined carefully.

The words "if there is nothing against them" (that is, if they are without reproach) means being without blame. It is the first qualification for elders mentioned by Titus (Titus 1:6). When we have determined that a deacon has no cause for blame, that is, that he is leading a Christ-honoring life, only then can he serve (literally, only then can he "deaconize").

Examine Their Families

"In the same way, their wives are to be women worthy of respect, not malicious talkers but temperate and trustworthy in everything. A deacon must be the husband of but one wife and must manage his children and his household well" (1 Tim. 3:11–12).

To whom was Paul referring in verse 11? "Wives" of deacons, as the

New International Version renders it? Or women in general (the word *gynē* can be used of either a woman or a wife)? Or did this word refer to what some have called "deaconesses," a woman's office in the church? Perhaps "wives" is preferable. Some interpreters say Phoebe was a deaconess (Rom. 16:1), but there seems to be no reason why the word *diakonon* in that verse should not be translated "servant" as it is elsewhere.

If Paul was speaking of deacons' wives, it is interesting that their behavior influenced the qualifications and worthiness of their husbands. Those wives must have earned respect (just as the deacons must have earned respect, 1 Tim. 3:8) and must not be malicious gossips. This latter expression is one word in the Greek, *diabolos,* which can mean anything from gossip to slander. We should not be surprised that deacons' wives should be both temperate and trustworthy.

Two more qualifications for deacons are given in verse 12—"a husband of but one wife" and able to "manage his children and his household well"—which are also to be true of elders (3:2, 4).

Examine Their Results

"Those who have served well gain an excellent standing and great assurance in their faith in Christ Jesus" (1 Tim. 3:13).

Two wonderful ideas surface in this verse. First, deacons who serve well receive an "excellent standing." The word rendered "standing" is *bathmos,* which appears only here in the New Testament. It speaks of gaining a reputation among fellow Christians (and might possibly refer to a step toward becoming an elder sometime in the future). Certainly the central issue here is character. Joe Stowell puts it this way: "Character still counts. In fact, in a society that minimizes values, the value of character escalates in terms of ministry. It is the shepherd who proves the point regarding the value and worth of character who becomes a trusted and readily followed leader. It is character that will be transferred to others and be used of God to transform lives."[5]

Deacons who fulfill their callings well also have a "great assurance," that is, confidence in relation to people and God. Churches do well to evaluate deacons—before they get into office as well as after.

In 1 Timothy 3:14–15 Paul stated his purpose in writing this letter to his young friend: he wanted to know how congregations should behave. "I am writing you these instructions so that . . . you will know how people ought to conduct themselves in God's household, which is the church of the living God, the pillar and foundation of the truth."[6]

Elders and deacons are the designated "hitters" in the church. Certainly others come up to bat game after game, and they might even have a better annual average or more home runs. But God has designated these officers as spiritual leaders in the church, and therefore they must meet high standards, specific spiritual qualifications.

CHAPTER 13
No Trash-Talking in the Huddle: Team Relationships

A STORY ON THE INTERNET tells about a boat race in which two teams practiced hard to reach peak performance. On the first day Team A won by a mile. So Team B hired a consultant to recommend a new strategy for the race. The consultant discovered that Team A had eight people rowing and one person steering while Team B had one person rowing and eight people steering. At a cost of $450,000, the consultant firm concluded that too many people were steering and not enough rowing.

As the race date approached the next year, Team B's management structure had been completely reorganized. The team now had four steering managers, three area steering managers, and a new performance review system for the one rower. That year Team A won by two miles. In abject humiliation the Team B corporation laid off the rower for poor performance and gave the managers a bonus for discovering the problem.

Sound familiar? Even churches and Christian organizations can become so bureaucratic, so organizationally top-heavy, that they stifle communication and community in essential ministry patterns. Or team morale can take a dive for other reasons. In any case enhancing team relationships becomes a major objective toward accomplishing the organization's mission.

BIBLICAL BACKGROUND: DAVID

Because leadership is invariably bound up in working with people, human relations take on great importance. Team leaders set the tone for team spirit. The presence they display in the organization largely determines the way people respond to tasks and how they view their roles.

David had no formal training in management practice, of course, but he certainly seems to have had a unique gift for administration. He responded with a positive sense of human relations in all aspects of his leadership. From obedience in his father's house to his aging presence on the throne, his sensitivity and concern for people were remarkable.

Relationship with Peers

When we think of human relations in leadership, we often think only of organizational layers. But effective leaders keep peer relations in order. After their clandestine meeting on the archery field, Jonathan said to his friend David, "Go in peace, for we have sworn friendship with each other in the name of the LORD, saying, 'The LORD is witness between you and me, and between your descendants and my descendants forever' " (1 Sam. 20:42). At that point, Jonathan was a prince, King Saul's son—and therefore he held a position much higher than David. But these young men thought of each other as peers.

Relationships with Supervisors

The sterling quality of David's character never showed greater brilliance than during the dark days when he was on the run from Saul. On at least two occasions, he had the opportunity to kill the king (1 Sam. 24 and 26), but it never occurred to him to do that. His respect for and faithfulness to Saul were evident, though the king was certainly undeserving of such loyalty.

David's behavior speaks to people who feel their bosses act unjustly toward them. How should they respond to injustice on the part of their supervisors? Look at the example of David. He said to Saul, "May the LORD judge between you and me. And may the LORD avenge the wrongs you have done to me, but my hand will not touch you. As the old saying goes, 'From evildoers come evil deeds,' so my hand will not touch you. Against whom has the king of Israel come out? Whom are you pursuing? A dead dog? A flea? May the LORD be our judge and decide between us. May he consider my cause and uphold it; may he vindicate me by delivering me from your hand" (24:12–15).

It is never proper for Christians to attempt to unseat leaders placed over us or to assume authority over them. Such politicized behavior is not worthy of God's children. We are to practice submission and to keep our own hearts right before God, leaving the results to Him.

Relationships with Staff

After the defeat of the Amalekites, some of David's less gracious men opposed giving any of the loot to those who had guarded their camp. But David's response echoed with characteristic kindness. "No, my brothers, you must not do that with what the LORD has given us. He has protected us and handed over to us the forces that came against us. Who will listen to what you say? The share of the man who stayed with the supplies is to be the same as that of him who went down to the battle. All will share alike" (1 Sam. 30:23–24).

Sometimes people in the front lines think and speak negatively of their officers, who seem to give all the orders and do none of the fighting. But David's troops held him in highest respect. On one occasion he planned to lead the army himself against the rebellious troops of Israel. Opposing that plan, they said, "You must not go out; if we are forced to flee, they won't care about us. Even if half of us die, they won't care; but you are worth ten thousand of us. It would be better now for you to give us support from the city" (2 Sam. 18:3). What pastor would not like to hear people praise him that way!

Relationships with Followers

Long before Peter Drucker wrote *The Effective Executive*,[1] David understood one of the basic tenets of that book: In relating to your followers, emphasize their strengths. Joab had many weaknesses, but he was a good soldier and a winning commander. Just as Abraham Lincoln put up with Ulysses S. Grant's drinking because Grant knew how to win battles, David put up with Joab's ruthlessness.

A blend of justice and grace forms David's pattern regarding Joab—and the pattern of God with humanity—and it is also a wise model for every leader.

ESTABLISHING CORE VALUES

William Pollard, chairman of the ServiceMaster Company, addresses the importance of values. "Servant leaders must be value-driven and performance-oriented. They must think through what is right and what is wrong in executing their responsibilities. They must lead people to do things the right way and to do the right things."[2]

Team relationships find their focus in three important areas: each team member's prior relationship to God; a mutual commitment to the mission; and a consensus and conviction regarding core values. Core values relate to our doctrinal beliefs as well as to the basic standards we expect from other Christians and ourselves. We feel deeply about these ideas because they stem from our purpose or mission.

I believe the following six core values ought to be held by all evangelical leaders.

The Gospel

Evangelical theology struggles today with issues like universalism and the true nature of Christ. Against those controversies, raging not only on the fringes but sometimes deep within what we would consider evangelical denominations, we must stand for the gospel, the only gospel, once delivered to the saints. As Paul affirmed so strongly in the Book of Galatians, there is no other gospel, no second choice, no substitute, no alternative. The place of the Cross and the empty tomb, and the necessity of the substitutionary atonement of Christ for eternal salvation, must drive all of us in our devotion to the Savior. The gospel is much more than a Christian flag waving over church or school; it represents individual and corporate commitment to God's commands and His Word. As workers are committed to these core values, their own relationships as team workers deepen.

Glory

Everything we do ought to bring glory to God. Work should bring glory to God; games should bring glory to God; relationships should bring glory to God; and church involvement should bring glory to God.

Grace

In evangelical churches and families, ambition gives way to submission, selfishness submits to grace. Believers are to exhibit grace in all their relationships. They show forgiveness; they exercise the freedom to be different, and for others to be different; they understand and utilize genuine flexibility. In a word, they are the least judgmental people on earth for they remember the grace God has extended to them.

Godliness

We talk a lot about excellence in behavior because the closer we get to God, the closer we get to excellence. Shoddiness and second-rate work in our efforts to serve God should be shunned. Of course, excellence does not mean perfection, but rather doing the very best we can with the resources God has given us. When we each pursue godliness, our team relationships are enhanced.

Gratitude

How thankful we should be for those who have brought us to where we stand today. Sacrificial parents, Christian leaders, teachers who worked for substandard wages. These ingredients form an integral part of our lives. As we stand on the banks of tomorrow, we might take a quick look back to see where we have been and, standing by Samuel's Ebenezer, cry out in gratitude, "Thus far has the LORD helped us" (1 Sam. 7:12). Being grateful to the Lord and to each other strengthens our relationships with other team members.

Gentleness

A few years ago we heard about a "kinder and gentler America." But those good words from the lips of former president George Bush hardly characterize our barbaric and violent times. Somehow in the midst of a culture gone berserk, evangelical congregations must appear in the desert of paganism to flow as oases of refreshment and gentleness in which people of all levels constantly demonstrate Spirit-guarded courtesy to one another. As Paul urged us, "Therefore, as God's chosen people, holy and dearly loved, clothe yourselves with compassion, kindness, humility, gentleness, and patience. Bear with each other and forgive whatever grievances you may have against one another. Forgive as the Lord forgave you. And over all these virtues put on love, which binds them all together in perfect unity" (Col. 3:12–14).

ENCOURAGING CREATIVE FOLLOWERSHIP

Traditionally we have thought of leadership as gifted people with special traits taking charge of the rest of us in order to make sure things get done. However, the recent theme—"the learning organization"—is much more in keeping with the New Testament. It centers on influencing everyone in the organization to achieve at a higher level. Steven Bornstein and Anthony Smith reject the earlier "industrial paradigm": "We submit that leadership in the future will more closely reflect a process whereby a leader pursues his or her vision by intentionally seeking to influence others and the conditions in which they work, allowing them to perform to their full potential and thus both increasing the probability of realizing the vision and maximizing the organizational and personal development of all parties involved."[3]

Creative leaders not only model innovation; they also inspire effective followership throughout the organization. Consider at least four ingredients of such creative followership, adapted from Thomas Gillmore's significant book, *Making a Leadership Change.*[4]

Shared Goals

This subject comes up so often in a book like Gillmore's that the repetition alone should highlight its importance. People who form a leadership team must be headed in the same direction, whether they are going down a football field or out to evangelize a community. People who do not share the goals and vision of ministry cannot exercise creative followership, or, for that matter, creative leadership.

Solid Feedback

Too many of us place all the responsibility for communication on the boss. When bosses seem noncommunicative, we tend to blame them for our struggles. But creative followers should take the initiative in communications by providing solid feedback. Here are the words of Marshall Goldsmith: "How will the leader of tomorrow differ from the leader of yesterday? . . . The effective leader of the future will consistently and efficiently *ask, learn, follow up,* and *grow.* The leader who cannot keep learning and growing will soon become obsolete in tomorrow's ever-changing world."[5] Team relationships are strengthened as leaders and followers communicate.

Strong Credibility

Repeatedly I have emphasized trust as a major leadership ingredient. People cannot follow someone they do not trust. But trust works two ways. Leaders generally do not release authority and responsibility to people whose credibility for competence and reliability may be shaky. *We enhance team relationships when we distribute leadership across the organization and provide empowerment to others.*

Everything we say about the credibility and capability of leaders applies to the work and ministry of creative followers, in most cases leaders themselves. Dave Ulrich says that all leaders should be "less concerned with saying what they will deliver and more concerned with delivering what they have said they would. . . . Consistent, reliable, predictable delivery on promises [is] the foundation of leadership."[6]

KEEPING TEAM SPIRIT FRESH

The obvious benefits of long tenure in a ministry organization are sometimes offset by staleness of spirit and a business-as-usual posture. While all of us ought to counteract such a potentially threatening attitude, generating new enthusiasm often falls to those in leadership roles. Sometimes changing a person's responsibilities will help, but that has somewhat limited boundaries. Six factors can help inject freshness in a leadership team.

Expectation

Think of that word from either direction—what the team leader expects of team members, or what they expect of him. Now add a third dimension—what each of us expects of ourselves in a growing organization. Sometimes false expectations need to be corrected. People joining Christian organizations often expect utopia. Believers, however, do not check their old natures at the door when signing contracts or taking ministry positions.

Cooperation

Although leaders may not be held responsible for everything that goes on in an organization, people do count on them to foster positive interpersonal relations. If an aura of distrust and hostility prevails in a Bible class, for example, we look to the teacher who allows such a negative learning atmosphere to persist. What kind of practical things can we do to keep relationships based on a spirit of civility and cooperation?
- Give people important work to do on critical issues.
- Give people autonomy over their tasks and resources.
- Give people visibility and recognition.

- Give people access to resources and individuals who can help them utilize those resources.

When we give work to a team that can be done better by individuals, or when we call people a team but manage them as individuals, we set them up for major losses.

Interaction

Leaders who want to keep team spirit fresh figure out ways to bring people together for something other than crisis intervention or problem-solving. When they do come together, those leaders use open dialogue to communicate clearly. They help people network effectively outside the team meetings—and they never allow trash-talking in the huddle.

Motivation

Motivation arises in a climate of trust, an atmosphere in which people feel secure. It grows when leaders are open about their own mistakes and struggles, a posture we often call "vulnerability." People committed to service in a ministry organization want to focus on gains and strengths; they want us to trust them enough to allow them to fail in pursuit of a noble goal. Remember, we don't motivate people by locker-room speeches at halftime. In one sense we can't motivate people at all. Cormack captures the best thrust of research on motivation in one clear paragraph: "Motivation comes from within. You cannot 'motivate' someone; this popular misconception causes much confusion. What is motivation? It consists of the feelings and attitudes we experience when a situation triggers one or more of our basic needs. This emphasis on situation is important since it means that either the leader or the member can create situations in which they or others will be motivated."[7]

Communication

Good leaders know the link between communication and motivation. A leader's comments have enormous impact on how team members feel about their positions, their teams, and their work. Positive conversation goes a long way toward lifting team spirit. I like the way William Plamondon put it: "When it comes to communicating with employees, I have never viewed communication as merely sharing information but as sharing responsibility. Rather than telling people what to do, I ask them what needs to be done and then do my best to remove any obstacles in their way. This not only generates the best ideas but also gives people a stake in the success of effort. One of our customer service representatives put it best when she said, 'If you want me to be there for the crash landing, you'd better invite me to the launch.' "[8]

Evaluation

Evaluation aimed at improving team efforts can be a morale booster. The bad rap that evaluation often gets stems not from its necessity, but from the way we handle it. Here's a quick and easy checklist to help improve your evaluation of your leadership team.

- Do you carry out informal evaluation throughout the year rather than letting everything rest on annual written forms?
- Do you set clear performance standards understood by each team member?
- Do you follow each written review with a personal discussion of both high-level performance and need for improvement?
- Do you set goals for the coming year at each annual evaluation?
- Do you allow team members to evaluate you?

Try fine-tuning your evaluation process until you can respond to each of those questions with a strong yes.

USING LEADERSHIP INFLUENCE

How should people respond when they are "promoted" from team member to team leader? In almost all situations this should be a positive move if one has maintained satisfactory relationships with peers and kept the lines of communication open. Our new leadership influence should never make us forget what we learned as group members and how well we know the struggles in the trenches. In an article in the fairly new publication *Team Management Briefings* an author suggests, "The first thing you should do is call your team together and explain the new relationship. Say something like, 'As a team leader, I'm expected to handle things differently from the way I did when I was a team member. Sometimes I'm going to have to make decisions that some of you won't like. It means that sometimes I'll have to talk to you about your performance, or turn down vacation requests, or support policies that aren't popular. I may even have to support the upper-management decisions that the team doesn't like. There will be times when it won't be easy for any of us, but I think it's important to put on the table the way things have changed, so we can all make the adjustment.' "[9]

Of crucial importance in leadership influence is recognition of where it comes from, what may be called "the sources of power." And let's remember a major axiom here: *The only way you effectively empower other people is by giving them some of yours.* What's involved in using influence (power) to enhance team relationships? Remember that influence often comes from a variety of sources; we work to divert those streams to other team members rather than channeling them into our own reservoirs.

Influence Comes to Those Who Have Needed Resources

The congregation may pay little attention to a deacon who happens to own a construction company until the church enters a building program. Now all of a sudden, his experience, expertise, and contacts make him an influential person in the church. We steer resources to developing team members by putting them in contact with anyone who can help make their ministries more effective.

Influence Comes to Those Who Can Help with Problems

The more critical the problem, the more important the resource. Let's expand our illustration from the preceding paragraph. Having begun a building program, the church runs into zoning problems when told by the city that a land-use requirement demands more parking than it appears they can create with the available space. Now the influence spotlight moves from the deacon in construction to a church member who has legal expertise in zoning issues.

Influence Comes to People Who Are Visible

For seven years my son served as assistant pastor for Christian education at a church in Houston. Almost as an afterthought he was asked to lead the music program as well, and so he carried both responsibilities during most of the time he served that church. We all know that a pastor of Christian education gets lost in the shuffle because so much of what he does is behind the scenes. But a music director shows up in every service, and that exposure lends important credibility and support to the Christian education program. People need visibility to advance in leadership, and this is one of the easiest forms of "power" for us to distribute. We need to take ourselves out of the lineup and insert other people, cheering loudly every time they make a good play.

Influence Comes to People Who Have Connections

For many team members in churches and Christian organizations, much of ministry work occurs behind the scenes. These team workers achieve influence by networking, knowing people whose connections and contacts, knowledge and expertise can assist them in achieving their own ministry goals. Secretaries, by the way, are usually wonderful at this skill.

Enhancing team relationships allows for no trash-talking in the huddle, or, for that matter, out on the field or the court. The team locks arms, kneels shoulder to shoulder, and moves forward together—or they don't move forward at all. The wonderful Greek word *homothymadon* ("together with one mind or purpose") is used several times in the Book of Acts to describe the unity, the team spirit, of the early church (see, for example, Acts 1:14; 2:1, 46; 4:24; 5:12).[10]

Community deals essentially with that intricate web of relationships that builds unity in a body of people. The term is used of more than a single staff or congregation, but the central idea holds true. In the words of Margaret Wheatley and Myron Kellner-Rogers, "Belonging together is defined by a shared sense of purpose. . . . The call of that purpose attracts individuals but does not require them to shed their uniqueness. Staying centered on what the common work is, rather than on single identities, transforms the tension of belonging and individuality into an energetic and resilient community."[11]

CHAPTER 14
Coaching Is the Key: Team Process

Bouncing back from heart surgery, coach Dan Reeves of the Atlanta Falcons led his team through the playoffs and right into the 1999 Super Bowl, earning the honor "NFL Coach of the Year." Reeves has spent most of his adult life in coaching, serving on the staffs of the Dallas Cowboys and the Denver Broncos, among other teams. But his example at Atlanta stands as a leadership model of coaching, teaching teamwork to a group of players whose ranks included few superstars.

The athletic metaphor is more than just a word picture in this book. Teaching teamwork has similar characteristics, whether it is carried out in a context of sports or church ministry. And the example of excellence offered by Ezra set the standard two and a half millennia ago.

BIBLICAL BACKROUND: EZRA

Ezra requested permission to go from Babylon to Jerusalem in order to teach the Scriptures there. He went in the year 475 B.C., thirteen years before Nehemiah. God sent him to call people to spiritual revival through serious study and preaching of the Scriptures. Ezra 7:10 offers some significant insights into the process of Ezra's ministry, perhaps giving the key to the spiritual success he experienced in his life and teaching. "For Ezra had prepared his heart to seek the Law of the LORD, and to do it, and to teach [its] statutes and ordinances in Israel" (NJKV).

Preparation

How significant to read that Ezra first prepared his heart before he attempted to carry on public ministry! Christians who seriously want to evaluate their call must sooner or later be led to examine their motives. Why do they serve? What is their underlying concern?

Ezra 7:6 indicates that Ezra was a "teacher well versed in the Law of Moses," which means he was skilled in the work of interpreting and teaching Scripture. Apparently he had prepared not only devotionally and spiritually, but mentally and professionally as well. This is a great example for church leaders in our day.

Perception

After Ezra had prepared his heart, he actively sought out the Law of the Lord. In other words, before he began to *teach* the Scriptures, he made sure that he *knew* the Scriptures. No doubt because of this skilled approach to his ministry, he also knew the people to whom God called him, understood the context of his teaching task, and had some clear-cut objectives regarding what he proposed to achieve in the restored city.

Sometimes we think that years of ministry experience qualify us for competence. Of course, experience is important. But if we have only practiced bad habit patterns all those years, we may be less qualified now than when we began.

Performance

No doubt Ezra was watched by the people to whom he ministered. They carefully noted whether their scribe practiced the Law of God in his own life or only verbalized it in public meetings. As they observed him, they noted a consistency between his words and his life. Not only did he seek God's truth; he observed (obeyed) it. Centuries later James emphasized this same point: "Do not merely listen to the word, and so deceive yourselves. Do what it says" (James 1:22).

Perpetuation

Ezra 7:10 tells us that Ezra prepared his heart to teach. This was his primary purpose in going to Jerusalem. He was neither a political leader like Zerubbabel nor a construction supervisor like Nehemiah. It would have been out of Ezra's character, call, and gifts for him to have taken on such responsibilities. We need people in our churches today who, like Ezra, are willing to let a task fall on their shoulders and agree to see it through to the end, to use their spiritual gifts for God's glory.

The order of these steps in Ezra's life is significant. *Preparation* of the heart precedes *perception* of the truth, which, in turn, gives birth to *performance* in life; only then can we expect *perpetuation* through teaching. Ezra gives us an outstanding example of an effective leader-coach.

DESIGNING PRESEASON WORKOUTS

Coaching begins long before the playing season starts. In early spring, football teams hit the field, getting back into shape and working on plays, even though the first scrimmage game probably won't take place until August. And those drills, those workouts that make game action possible, begin to mold players into a team, regardless of their positions. What traits do we try to develop in churches and Christian organizations? What tools do we want to put in the hands of people so they can be more effective? Consider the following five.

Importance

Only a few players end up at quarterback or shooting guard; the rest learn their roles and, on an effective team, function in those roles. Once again, all this goes back to our mission. We help people believe in the potential and value of their roles and tasks as we explain how those roles and tasks serve the mission of the church organization. When players get wrapped up only in what they themselves do rather than how their roles function in relationship to everyone else on the team, their effectiveness rapidly begins to dwindle.

In his years with the three-time national champion Chicago Bulls, Scott

Kerr, in the sixth-man position, came off the bench when the team needed a three-point shot to boost their scoring. He didn't lead the team in scoring, rebounding, or assists, but his key role as an essential bench player helped the Bulls significantly. We need to give more consideration to "bench strength" in Christian organizations.

Flexibility

In the past decade or so we have seen a change in business and industry in the way people handle their work time. Some people work out of their homes, staying in touch with a central office by e-mail and fax machines. Others work in a car with a cellular phone, as they travel from point to point making business contacts.

But the church has rarely kept up with flexibility in ministry options. We design a program, decide how many people we need to staff it, then draft players to fill the positions. Sometimes those players receive very little coaching or none at all. Sometimes they serve out of neurotic compulsion to duty rather than the joy of playing a particular position of significance to the whole team. The effective church of the twenty-first century may discover that flexibility in the ministry menu will determine not only how many people choose to serve, but how well they do it.

Reputation

Many people wondered why John Elway, the Denver Broncos' quarterback, returned to football after winning the Superbowl in 1998. Those questions faded away as the Broncos won the 1999 Superbowl and Elway received the "Most Valuable Player" trophy. On display throughout the crucial season, Elway understood, as he had throughout his career, that he needed to carry out his job with excellence, to continue to live up to his reputation.

The Bible emphasizes this often. When the seven servants were chosen (Acts 6:2–6), their essential spiritual qualifications were further refined by the need for public recognition. In other words, the apostles required the seven to have a reputation for godliness and faith. "Choose seven men from among you who are *known* to be full of the Spirit and wisdom" (6:3, italics added). Simply assuming that these internal qualities were in place was not enough. Research indicates that people are motivated by reputation, a personal awareness that others recognize what they do in serving the Lord.

Knowledge

I've often wondered in recent years why it took professional leadership studies so long to come around to this theme. Perhaps the so-called knowledge explosion elevated the necessity of ongoing coaching in almost every organization. Yet, as I have said earlier in this book, the church is an obvious learning organization. One can hardly imagine anyone serving in any ministry who is not learning week in and week out to function better as a Christian leader. This assumes, of course, that effective coaching is supporting the team all along the way. We should be encouraged, too, that in an age of emphasis on music styles, huge buildings, and megachurches, solid Bible teaching still draws people wherever they find it.

Achievement

Coaches know that teams can't win games unless player rewards are based on measurable results. Nobody becomes captain simply by hanging around for a few years. A track star at the Olympics who wins the gold medal in the four-hundred-meter run may very well raise his hands to the sky and shout, "I did it." But the ultimate test in team leadership is for people to say after successful ministry accomplishment, "We did it together!"

Something else goes on in those preseason workouts—a group of players learns to function as a team. In motivation a sense of belonging is crucial to a willingness to serve, to learn, and to grow. As Tom Phillips explains, "The placement of each person in a team is vital. As the body of Christ, no member of the team is less important than another, or more important than another. People are gifted for specific kinds of service and usually grow through experience in ability, discernment, and wisdom for future and greater levels of service."[1]

GETTING THE TEAM'S ATTENTION

Spring training isn't worth much if people don't apply themselves and listen to their coaches. Annually, on an athletic field and in churches, leaders must bring something fresh, some new wrinkle in old plays or better yet, new plays replacing old ones that didn't work very well. Team leaders can bring that freshness to a ministry organization in several ways.

Fresh Voices

Sometimes people hesitate to get involved, wondering whether a new approach may just be the old leadership style in some deceitful form. It may take awhile to get people enthusiastic about playing on a team, but sincere commitment to this approach will capture attention.

Fresh Vocabulary

Freshness comes when words like *togetherness, teamwork,* and *dialogue* replace words like *duty* and *requirements*. This can help gel team spirit and can encourage each worker. "There is no substitute for effective communication within the team."[2]

Fresh Perspectives

Thousands of people in evangelical churches hold narrow and often distorted perspectives on ministry. They see their ministries as necessary only to keep the church doors open and help present programs survive. They lack a sense of call; they lack a clear vision. And they lack the essential perspective to see the whole playing field and the significance of everyone on it. Expanding team workers' perspective for ministry usually takes awhile, but it is needed if the team is to be a winning team.

Fresh Passion

Christian leaders should often ask themselves, "What leads people to support what we have said we will do?" The answer is passion, the emotional side of strategy. Strategy without passion is cold and unattractive; passion without strategy can be wild, noisy, and unproductive. But hand in hand, these two shine like stars on a dark night, attracting the attention of anyone who wants to look up.

Fresh Ideas

Ministry leaders dare not let the quest for effectiveness drive out experimentation. When we view leadership as coaching, we give people the opportunity to serve in different positions, to try new ideas, to respond positively to developing their own leadership abilities. Interestingly business and industry leaders don't give their companies very high marks on developing leadership capacity throughout the organization. "According to a recent Conference Board survey of 400 of the *Fortune 1,000* companies, only 8 percent of executives rated their firms' overall leadership capacity as excellent. Forty-four percent rated their leadership capacity as good, and an alarming 49 percent of companies earned a fair or poor rating."[5] Managers in those companies ranked specific aspects of leadership tasks rather poorly; they rated their companies as 30 percent effective in "building teams," 40 percent effective in "teaching from honest mistakes," and 32 percent effective on "managing creative talent."

I doubt that those four hundred companies can compete as well as they would like in the *Fortune 1,000* climate if those scores hold up very long. Experimental leadership, challenging the process over and over again, will capture people's attention in any learning organization, including the church.

NAMING THE LINEUP

Larry Green, senior pastor-teacher of Northland Bible Church in Grand Rapids, has developed a fine three-step program to develop team members and get people into the right place. I offer those steps here with my own comments, but first here are Green's words. "Believing that every member is a minister uniquely designed by God, and believing that the task of pastoral ministry is to equip all members to minister in harmony with their unique designs, the question then follows: How do I effectively match minister and ministries?"[4]

Assess Their Maturity

In ministry, spiritual maturity comes to mind immediately when we talk about "naming the lineup." But social, emotional, and intellectual maturity is important too. And let's not expect the same levels at every position. The Bible gives us strong reason to believe that we should require more from elders and deacons than from ushers and youth sponsors. As we put ministry players into position, we do well to remember that a vast segment of church problems arises from immaturity.

Assist Their Discovery

This spins off the comments above about freshness. And it reminds us again of our role as a learning organization. Let's not limit the question to, "Are people learning more about the Bible while growing spiritually?" Let's also ask whether they are discovering their own gifts and calls from God to serve in important positions on the team.

Assign Their Ministry

Keeping in mind the flexibility factor already discussed in this chapter, this step involves putting the right people in the right places—in ministries for which they have both interest and a sense of calling. Obviously the role of coaching continues central in the process. As Leighton Ford puts it, "If we want to raise up leaders like Jesus who have a clear voice and his strong and compelling touch, those of us who are called to develop them need to embody the same. We need to have a clear message of what leadership is. We also need to touch them with our prayers and time and character and involvement. This is a costly involvement, but one that will affirm them and help them become all God has called them to be."[5]

PREPARING FOR A GAME

Just as a good basketball coach knows how to get his team ready for action, so a good spiritual leader knows how to prepare his workers for ministry.

Field the Best Team

We already talked about the lineup, but each contest may require a slight variation. One year I played the sixth-man position on a basketball team, and when a game started I had no idea how soon I would break into the lineup or what I would be asked to do. But I knew the coach wanted the best team on the floor at any given moment in the game, and he wanted to be sure we knew our purpose as a group. He trained us to play our positions; he showed us how to be serious at practice; and he gave us resources for solving problems on the floor. This is a good idea for any ministry leader.

Know Your Players

You can't field the best team unless you know the skills of the players. Sometimes coaches have to play people without wide experience. Maybe an injury forces the use of a player who needed a few more weeks of seasoning in practice. But that's all part of coaching. And when those times come, coaches not only make important decisions; they also teach players how to make good decisions. So it is in any ministry organization; leaders must know the skills of their workers and make proper decisions.

Call the Plays

Very rarely in basketball is play-calling done on the floor. Sometimes a point guard will initiate a play, but more likely he gets signals from the coach and passes the play to his team members while bringing the ball down the floor. Most of that is done in hand signals, of course, but hand signals are useless if players on the floor don't understand the play. Communication permeates every aspect of coaching. H. B. London, Jr., reminds us of the need for good communication in working with our ministry teams. "Most leaders have little problem speaking, but severe limitations when it comes to listening. A majority of the problems we face in the church occur because we usually communicate on a 'me' level. Sometimes we fall victim to conflict because we do not have a common vocabulary: We do not know how to describe what we are seeing and feeling without initiating an argument."[6]

Make Good Substitutions

When you pull your sixth man off the bench and move him in to point guard, you need confidence that he knows what's expected. Coaching assumes that people can achieve at increasingly higher levels. Good coaches encourage people to develop through feedback, to make changes in their lives and skills as challenges require. The whole coaching system rests on an assumption of skill improvement, a covenant of accountability, and a system of rewards.

Follow the Game Plan

How often we hear sports announcers say, "No matter what the defense does, the coach is going to stick with his game plan." To be sure, if you're down twenty points with less than two minutes to go, it may be time to change the game plan and try a few drastic revisions. But generally we have strategies for service and strategies for developing leaders in service. The game plan should be broad enough to allow for the following ingredients:
- making sure the players know how to handle their positions
- constantly keeping them informed
- helping them know where the problems are and how to solve them
- consistently widening the team's perspective as the game develops.

When recruiting players, it may be prudent to select the best player in the draft. On a basketball team, for example, you may need a tall center, but if a great small forward is available, you may want to grab him and revise the makeup of the team to fit him in. Let's not just design empty slots and then try to find people who fill those positions. Instead, let's focus on people and then design ministries that will allow them to use their God-given gifts and talents in serving the Lord.

FACILITATING BETTER PLAY

Most team sports have a halftime during which adjustments can be made. Coaches and players come together for an intense and important discussion of what went well and what went wrong during the first half. The goal is better team play in the second half. Applying that to Christian ministry, leaders, as coaches, should direct their attention to three crucial areas.

In Ourselves

Effective coaches develop self-awareness, an understanding of needs, and a picture of the way other players actually see the game. It's not accidental that both offensive and defensive coordinators of football teams sit high up in the press boxes so they can see the entire field. Leaders need to understand how well their own playing skills develop, but more importantly, how their teammates handle their roles and function together. And that takes us to the next level.

In Our Leadership Team

Here we move to interpersonal relations. We work with volunteers in the church by using empathetic listening, advising, and counseling, and, perhaps most of all, encouraging. We remind them of the importance and uniqueness of team play and point out how easy it is to misunderstand team leadership. Jon Katzenbach has developed a list of what he calls "ten myths of team leadership," which I have paraphrased here.

1. The primary leader determines whether a team is successful or not.
2. The primary leader must make all the key decisions.
3. A team is a team because we call it a team.
4. If every team member is in the right place, teams will emerge.

5. The top team is responsible for fulfilling the mission.
6. Teamwork at the top will lead the team performance throughout the organization.
7. Teamwork requires many unusually lengthy meetings.
8. Winning teams have heavily involved primary leaders.
9. Team members must spend nonwork hours socializing with each other.
10. Teams at the top must serve as role models.[7]

Many church leaders readily believe many of these myths. Yet how essential it is to develop a serving team, a working group whose performance will improve because we coach them effectively.

In the Entire Organization

Remember the various components of any ministry role—leadership, environment, mission, task, and organization. Each church or ministry organization has its own culture, and its players must be coached in a manner consistent with that personality. That's why we say leadership is situational; you deal with the people you have in the organization which you serve without trying to bend everything in order to make it fit you.

CHAPTER 15
Changing Team Captains: Leadership Transition

THE FOUNDING PASTOR of a local church has served that congregation for twenty years. He literally hand-selected the first elders and has been the only pastor many congregants in that church have known. Now, at the age of fifty, he senses God's call to foreign missionary service and has announced his resignation. The church faces an organizational vacuum since the congregation has never before experienced the process of calling and installing a new leader.

Meanwhile across the city a college is going through the same process. A long-term president has announced his retirement, and the board faces its most pressing task. However, things are very different on that campus. Many of the board members, experienced business and educational leaders, have been through resignations and retirements throughout their careers. Rather than a vacuum, a political quagmire has developed in which two vice presidents are jockeying for consideration, the president wishes to advance the name of his own son as successor, and the chairman of the search committee has his own personal agenda regarding the research process.

Changing team captains is never easy, and in Christian organizations it is often done with inadequate and even hurtful techniques. This important process needs to be addressed.

BIBLICAL BACKGROUND: ELIJAH

All of a sudden Elijah appeared on the scene at the beginning of 1 Kings 17. We learn only that he was a Tishbite living in Gilead and was sent by God to confront the wicked King Ahab. Elijah's name means "Yahweh is God," and we assume that he was born at Tishbe in the territory of Naphtali.

Elijah's ministry spanned approximately two decades in very difficult times in Israel's history. He certainly had his ups and downs just as leaders do today, and he shows us how God can use a person of stark humanness in such outstanding and miraculous ways. No wonder James could write that Elijah "was a man just like us. He prayed earnestly that it would not rain, and it did not rain on the land for three and a half years" (James 5:17). With that example James encouraged New Testament believers to be faithful in prayer.

Leaders must learn to transfer the mantle. Part of the twenty or so years Elijah served in the public eye was spent rather quietly, particularly the period during the wars between Ahab, king of Israel, and Ben-Hadad, king of Syria. The prophet made only one appearance to Ahab in his reign, and that was to rebuke the king for the murder of Naboth (1 Kings 21:17–29). God also used Elijah to tag his successor, Elisha (19:16, 19–21).

The two prophets spent approximately ten years together (from about 860 to 850 B.C.). During that time we assume that Elijah taught Elisha everything he knew about prayer, about preaching, about hiding from—and confronting—wicked kings, and about faith in the God of Israel. Elisha had only one final request when it became apparent that his mentor would be taken away: "Let me inherit a double portion of your spirit" (2 Kings 2:9).

Ten years before he left the scene Elijah began grooming his successor. He did not know how soon God would take him, and therefore he wisely used every minute he had with the new prophet. From a study of the ministry of Elisha in 2 Kings, we see that his teacher did the job well.

WHEN ARE NEW LEADERS READY?

Before answering this question, let's review what elsewhere I have called "Pitfalls in Leadership Selection."

1. *Availability bias.* Sadly, many Christian organizations ask three basic questions when a leadership position becomes available: Who's handy? Who's visible? Who's cheap? Certainly a handy, visible, and inexpensive leader may also be competent and long-term, but that is not likely. Availability bias betrays laziness in our processes of leadership recruitment and development.

2. *Association bias.* This refers to some connection with existing leadership. It might just be a long-term relationship, such as a pastor recommending to the official board that a youth pastor who has served the church for five years now be appointed associate pastor. In its ugliest form, association bias deteriorates into nepotism. We have all seen it—Christian organizations passed on from father to son or husband to wife as though they were family businesses. Certainly strong relational leaders draw followers. And people closely associated to the present leader may be the logical selections for leadership needs. But it can be a pitfall, a danger zone. Keeping "power" within the family may be typical of Old Testament monarchical times, but we find no evidence whatsoever of such behavior in the New Testament.

3. *Agreement bias.* Here the present leader asks, "Who's like me? Who thinks like I do? Who won't rock the boat? Who won't change what we've developed here in our organization?" Like availability and association, agreement hardly represents a mortal sin. In some situations, agreement may be essential (for example, in doctrinal matters). But if we follow the leadership principle "lead to your strength and staff to your weakness," it may very well be wise for leaders to find those who have some differences and disagreements in order to help the organization toward its future.[1]

Maturity

Immaturity, especially in a leadership role, can quickly bring a church or Christian organization into collapse. In writing about "spotting a new leader," Fred Smith says he looks for such things as leadership in the past, willingness to take responsibility, mental toughness, peer respect, and the capacity to create or catch vision.[2] All these (and others he lists) reflect a maturity capable of handling the task for which one is being considered.

Management

A church or other ministry organization cannot afford to hire someone whose rhetorical skills or fund-raising capabilities obscure an inability to plan, organize, lead, and supervise. According to Olan Hendrix, "Local churches usually train people to teach, sing, and usher. They rarely train for managing. Yet it is the absence of management skills and tools that causes most of our problems. A church leader once told me he heard this 'management stuff' all week at work and wanted nothing to do with it at church. Management is needed in all organizations, secular and religious, whenever people attempt to work together."[3]

Influence

In looking for a new leader, Christian organizations ought to consider what other leaders have influenced their candidate directly. What leadership style will he emulate, either intentionally or subconsciously? Whom does she consider an effective leader, one who meets biblical standards?

New leaders usually become models for other people in ministry organizations. In Christian leadership we look to the Lord for the primary demonstration of what we should be, and then we reflect that image to others.

Call

Ezekiel 3:4–9 reveals how strongly God wanted Ezekiel to understand his call to ministry. The message from heaven repeats the theme that Ezekiel was not sent to some exotic foreign mission field, but to his own people. This was not his choice; it was God's. I imagine the one thing that sustained Ezekiel during those dark hours of rejection and the distortion of his message by his own people was the recognition that God had called him and that God would therefore sustain him in the task.

God's words to Ezekiel could help sustain any new pastor or president in difficult times. Long tenure (staying power) affords a major key to effective ministry. Nationally the tenure of college presidents runs just over five years on average and the tenure of pastors is considerably less than that. Boards of organizations looking for a new leader will want to be sure those leaders are called by God and are willing to stay until God calls them elsewhere.

Experience

When Paul met with the Ephesian elders at Miletus, they learned that he intended for them to lead as he did (Acts 20:28, 31). The strength of the churches Paul founded rested on the faithfulness of team leaders like the Ephesian elders. It's quite inconceivable that a church would call a pastor with no experience at all, and the board of a college should be looking for a leader who has held high-level responsibility even if he has not yet carried the title "president."

Training

In a top-level leadership post, experience and training should be like Siamese twins. Ideally training should precede experience, but they often occur simultaneously over a period of years. When we face a major leadership transition, we need both. Increasingly organizations are looking "in house" to find top leadership. But that will be possible only if they have intentionally cultivated leaders throughout the organization. In October 1997 the Motorola Finance Leadership Council and Arthur Andersen's Global Desk Practices Group released a report identifying forty business, government, and nonprofit organizations with effective leadership. They distilled their report into "Seven Practices for Effective Leadership Development." Here's one of those practices: "Create a proving ground for a potential leader. To grow professionally, people need to be challenged. At Shell, for instance, future leaders selected for the company's 'value creation teams' undertake demanding new projects in addition to their on-going duties. This forces them to learn time-management and delegation—essential leadership skills—as well as to produce results."[4]

Dependability and accountability could also be mentioned, but those qualities are both obvious and subsumed in the list above. Clearly, when conducting a leadership search, we do not want to land candidates who are not ready for the post we need to fill.

WHAT CLIMATE IS MOST CONDUCIVE TO NEW LEADERSHIP?

Two books on leadership training dominate the horizon. In the secular domain Thomas Gillmore's *Making a Leadership Change* offers value from cover to cover,[5] and in the Christian realm Robert W. Dingman's *In Search of a Leader* is outstanding. Dingman's third chapter begins with this paragraph: "When the search committee is formed, half the damage is already done! That statement of mine may sound somewhat cynical, but it points out a truth that repeatedly asserts itself in search committees I have seen or heard about: Too often the leadership of an organization responds too quickly to the news of a need for a new leader."[6]

Dingman is correct. The governing body of a Christian organization searching for a new leader bears the responsibility of creating a climate conducive to the transition and friendly to the new team captain. Before describing that environment, let me emphasize that not all features are possible in every leadership search. Nevertheless they all merit our consideration, and, where we can make appropriate adjustments, we should attempt to have these components in place.

Clear Focus on the Mission

A board should always be in touch with the organization's mission, but never more directly than when its members contemplate new leadership. And that mission must be articulated in its most poignant detail to any candidate. "The starting point for answering the question of where the organization is going is to re-examine the mission statement of the organization. If you do not have such a document, perhaps this is the time to develop one. If the re-examination of your mission statement reveals that it is out-of-date or otherwise now inappropriate, re-casting it now is timely so that it points your organization in the correct direction even before you begin inviting someone to lead it."[7]

Strong Performance by the Predecessor

An organization in which strong leadership has prevailed for a number of years sets the platform for new and, by God's grace, even stronger leadership to carry on. But let's assume that the organization is struggling, deterioration has already set in, and the next leader will be viewed as a "rescue operation" if not a savior for survival. Now we have a situation in which a governing body can determine that it will not make the same mistake again. It can determine to build now for the next transition, though that may be several years in the future.

Early Announcement by the Departing Leader

Early in 1998 Jay Kesler announced he would step down as president of Taylor University in the year 2000. Taylor reached a high point in its history under Kesler's leadership, and as he reached retirement age, the school had every opportunity not only to build on strong performance but also to carry out a timely and effective transition to a new president. Contrast that with a pastor who has been secretly sending out résumés and, on acquiring a new position, notifies a shocked board that he will leave within a month. Certainly college presidencies are more difficult to fill than most pastorates, but early announcement can be helpful in both cases. Two years is certainly not too far in advance for a college president to announce his retirement, and for a pastor to announce his resignation six months to a year in advance is useful for a local church.

Frances Hesselbein has a great paragraph on this point. "Effective leaders plan an exit that is as positive and graceful as their entrance was. They come to the job committed to the mission and goals of the organization and to their personal goals, with a sense of where they want the organization to be and where they want to be personally when they leave. When those goals are realized, the transition to new leadership becomes a primary focus. It becomes, literally, the ultimate leadership responsibility."[8]

A Pleasant Exit

Making a pleasant exit can't always be guaranteed. Sometimes leaders are dismissed in a difficult situation. But even then, maturity can provide a graceful exit. People forced out of leadership positions need not make life miserable for everyone they leave behind. Having studied the personal effects of forced exits, John LaRue observes, "Put God in the mix, and a negative situation can lead to a number of positive results. For example, two-thirds of ousted pastors report that their faith and prayer life improved because of their trying experiences. On the home front, the majority say their ability to be a loving spouse and caring parent was enhanced. Even though a third of all pastors forced out have not yet returned to local church ministry, nearly half (48 percent) say their ordeal encouraged their sense of call to the pastorate."[9]

The outgoing leader does not always cause the unpleasantness of a forced exit. Sometimes boards and governing bodies corrupt the process so that a pleasant exit becomes nearly impossible. I have observed that the two most troublesome behaviors on the part of boards who dismiss leaders are *undue secrecy in the procedure* and *inadequate communication about the decision.*

Open Selection Process

In my view all stakeholder groups deserve a voice in the selection of a new leader. Yes, the bylaws may say that the board selects the president, the president selects the dean, and so forth, or that the church elders or congregation selects the pastor. But a president who dumps a dean on a faculty without consulting key faculty leaders or even elected officers in advance may be asking for trouble. A college board should have on its search committee one or more educators from the board, a representative faculty member, an alumni representative, and some means of listening to student voices.

Many denominations have useful systems for assisting a church in acquiring a new pastor. In some cases, however, a heavy-handed district superintendent or headquarters official may actually interfere with the needs and desires of a local congregation. Dingman describes both sides of the issue. "When the denominational system is well-tuned and you have an attentive resource person at headquarters who understands the needs of your congregation, denominational involvement comes as a gift from God. When the system malfunctions, is restrictive or inept and bureaucrats don't seem to care, such involvement can seem to be the creation of Satan himself. At this point, your spiritual nature needs to be tempered by practical experience."[10]

Extremes should be avoided here. There's probably no justification for a board appointment made secretly with a surprise announcement that drops a new leader on the staff and constituency. On the other hand, a congregational vote on every résumé represents a nonsensical waste of time. Let's keep the distinctions clear: *Voice, not necessarily vote,* makes for an open selection process.

The search committee should be active rather than passive, looking for candidates who meet their predetermined criteria rather than just stacking résumés. And no member of the search committee (or the boards) should allow his or her personal agenda to corrupt the selection process. Respect for the heritage of the church or organization should permeate the transition and the selection, but should not dominate the process.

WHY IS A SMOOTH TRANSITION SO IMPORTANT?

"In every succession, the organization's credibility, momentum, vision, and values are at risk. A poor transition can drain corporate energy and resources for years to come. Every ministry, regardless of its size or purpose, must carefully plan and execute the transition of leadership. Without a smooth succession, lasting success cannot be achieved."[11]

Several factors make for an effective transition, factors that take us back to the first two sections of this chapter.

Choose the Right Leader

While Elijah thundered against Ahab and Ahaziah, a young farmer with a similar name but a completely different background and temperament pushed a plow in the meadows of Abel Meholah. Imagine the drama of the moment as the legendary prophet of Mount Carmel quietly walked by the farm boy and threw his hairy cloak over Elisha's strong shoulders, a symbol that has never been mistaken from that time until this.

Elisha did not feel any pressure tactics, for he sensed that this was God's appointment. He knew that he was God's choice to follow Elijah in the prophetic lineup. So he burned the plow, butchered the oxen, and set out to spend the next fifty years as a cultivator of God's vineyard, "plowing" the hearts and minds of the people of Israel.

Too often today Christians are satisfied with mantles rather than supernatural power. Symbolism is not wrong, and Elisha began his ministry by dividing the rivers with a smack of the Tishbite's mantle. But eventually only the internal power of the energizing Spirit of God would sustain him in the hours of difficulty and testing. So it is with us.

Coach Immediate Staff

No one has more at stake in the selection of a new college president than the faculty and staff. True, the alumni and students have genuine interest, but the lives and ministries of all faculty and staff will be greatly influenced by the board's choice. That's why faculty and staff should be a part of the selection process, and why someone needs to work closely with them in the transition period. Indeed, several members of the faculty and staff need to be part of the transition team. It is appropriate and highly desirable for a candidate who has passed muster with the search committee to sit down with representatives of the faculty and staff for serious discussions regarding their acceptance and expectations of new leadership. In fact a candidate should insist on it.

Control Prearrival Factors

In facing a leadership transition, churches and Christian organizations need to stop and review both mission and vision. A common danger lies not in taking too long, but in jumping too soon. Veronica Biggins, an executive search consultant with Heidrick and Struggles, observes, "When a volunteer board faces a period without a chief executive, they tend to rush. It's easy for board members to panic, because they may be expected to step up and run the organization while they make a decision. Most board members don't want that responsibility, so they rush to get the position filled."[12]

Prearrival factors include most everything we've talked about so far, including the process itself. The example of Elijah with Elisha, while it affords a look at rapid transition, pales by comparison with Moses and Joshua, a situation in which prearrival factors were under control for forty years. As William Sanford LaSor notes, "Few men, if any, step into responsible positions without preparation. Sometimes in our shortsightedness we seem to get the idea in regard to Bible characters that they come on the scene ready-made, fully prepared; there they are, God's gift to the world! They take up the work, and that is all there is to it. But if you will read more carefully, you will find that usually—I think we could even say always—there is a period of preparation behind them. God lays His plans well in advance."[13]

Cope with Postarrival Factors

Postarrival factors include a cheerful welcome, a good solid beginning with staff, faculty, congregation, or constituency, building a new management team if that is necessary, some possible reorganization, and within the first year or two, some new thinking about vision and long-range planning.

Certainly we want to avoid some of the common sins of new leadership relationships such as heavy-handedness right from the start, dramatic changes without sufficient time to understand the present system, and the despicable practice of dismissing all staff members. Such a practice defies any biblical explanation and represents the worst secular management on display. Youth pastors, music directors, and other staff members can be called by God to serve in a given church just as much as the senior pastor. Their ousting at his departure makes no sense at all in team leadership, even though it may satisfy the autocratic style of imperious bosses.

Erickson offers seven guidelines new leaders can follow to help create positive postarrival environments.

- Preserving the dignity of the predecessor by speaking well of his record and accomplishments
- Being sensitive to the transition needs of the executive team
- Building a relationship with the board
- Determining to keep the values and vision that historically built the ministry
- Committing to a learning process
- Communicating face to face with the whole organization
- Following up on the network relationships of the incumbent.[14]

Sometimes, in the flexible wideness of God's grace, new leaders can overcome a predecessor's unpleasant exit and the sour climate of an organization left in ruin, by the way they present themselves, especially during that critical first year.

WHERE SHOULD WE WATCH FOR TRAPS?

Yes, relationships with the board will be crucial for the new leader, but the biggest traps lie in the path of connecting with existing staff. Here Gilmore offers sound advice. "Leaders, especially early in their tenure, do not get fully developed options from which they select a path. Rather, a direction begins to emerge from a sequence of choices—about people, issues, resources . . . and from serendipity. . . . Traps arise from misunderstandings and the inability to discuss the situation freely."[15]

Patterns of Delegation

I will never forget the first month of my years in one leadership post. An inauguration dinner had been planned, and a member of the planning committee came to my office to ask what color I preferred for the napkins at that event. I don't recall my verbal response; I want to think it was polite. But in my heart I wondered if a miasma of micromanagement lay before me.

This is what Gilmore means when he talks about the trap of delegation. Since most leaders inherit staff, those people may have been accustomed either to working independently or to asking for guidance on everything. New leaders face a mutual learning experience in order to provide a good working relationship within a reasonable amount of time. Since leaders early in their tenure do not want to appear unresponsive, they tend to give off signals suggesting they want involvement in everything. The result is an overloaded desk and staff relinquishing their independence—either eagerly or grudgingly.

Internal versus External Priorities

Suppose a new college president faces some immediate fund-raising tasks related to the general fund. Never mind new building programs; he needs to deal with a deficiency in last year's budget and the increased costs of operating the college during his first year. Following the advice of the advancement office, he heads out to strategic donors and is gone for two or three weeks at a time. The faculty may misunderstand his sense of priorities, feeling that he has committed himself to public relations and finance with little concern for the realities of academic life. He may soon discover the necessity to mend fences back home and learn to balance his time between internal and external priorities.

Handling Resistance to Change

In staff meetings a new pastor makes suggestions and asks for input. The staff responds, the elders get involved, and knowing the practical realities of the church, they often cite difficulties that the pastor's ideas might encounter. He interprets this feedback as resistance or a lack of vision. So he may then consult the staff and the elders on fewer matters. If that happens, they identify less with his ideas and become bystanders, no longer feeling that their own leadership is important.

According to Gillmore, traps are inevitable, but there are some strategies by which leaders can extricate themselves or even avoid the traps entirely.

1. Explicitly examine whether seemingly attractive goals or positive actions can contain unforeseen problems.
2. Be open to changing your mind.

3. Examine counter-intuitive possibilities.
4. Use networking to get fresh perspectives.
5. Invest in theorizing.[16]

Gillmore adds, "Behind many of the failed relationships between talented people in a transition is some misunderstanding like those described. The conclusion is usually the resignation or firing of the subordinate or, more rarely, the departure of a new leader. In either case, valuable human capital is lost."[17]

Think again of the new leader who replaced the prophetic icon, Elijah. Despite the striking similarities between their ministries and mannerisms, these two men were quite different. Elijah's miracles were spectacular, national, and highly visible, whereas Elisha dealt more often with little people and common things such as water, oil, pottage, loaves, and ax heads.

Elijah was an ascetic, a mountain man who thrived in the wilds by himself; but Elisha seemed to be always in the company of students from the schools of the prophets and apparently exercised some kind of leadership role among them.

The lesson here is simple—but so important. God calls His people to follow others who have served in the same capacity in earlier years. It is tempting to measure ourselves by the record of a predecessor, failing to realize that God does not expect us to be like anyone else. We must carry out the gifts and commands He has placed on us for our time. We can certainly learn from those who have gone before, but we ought not try to restrict God's powerful hand by mimicking the ministry of any other one of His servants.

EPILOGUE

AFTER I SPOKE RECENTLY at an educator's convention on leadership, a teacher came up to tell me about one of her students. This twelve-year-old (whom we'll call Jordan) is a seventh-grader with some verbal-skill problems. Jordan does well in all studies that don't require expressing ideas in writing.

One day the class was assigned the task of preparing several definitions of words describing godly behavior, including the word meekness. Jordan sat quietly behind his blank page until his teacher came to check on him. "I know what meekness is," he appealed, "but I can't describe it in words." The caring teacher invited her struggling student to express his ideas with pictures, and he beamed his approval of the idea. In minutes his paper reflected several unmistakable images: a boy helping a smaller child up steep steps; a boy taking out the trash for his mother; a boy sweeping the floor, smiling all the while.

That's what this book has tried to say—biblical leadership is primarily an attitude, a willingness to serve the Lord without greater recognition or applause. Christian leaders must focus on serving others, coaching their ministries toward excellence, because that is both the pattern and command of Jesus Christ. Biblical team leadership lives out the principle of Matthew 20:26, "Whoever wants to become great among you must be your servant."

ENDNOTES

PREFACE

1. Leighton Ford, *Transforming Leadership* (Downers Grove, Ill.: InterVarsity, 1991), 52.

CHAPTER 1—THE HEART OF A CHAMPION: LEADERSHIP ATTITUDES

1. William J. Drath, "Changing Our Minds about Leadership," *Issues and Observations* 16 (1996): 2 (italics his).
2. Allan Sloan, "The Hit Men," *Newsweek*, 26 February 1996, 44–46.
3. Ronald L. Enroth, *Churches That Abuse* (Grand Rapids: Zondervan, 1992), 103.
4. Drath, "Changing Our Minds about Leadership," 4.
5. John C. Maxwell, "Practices of Leadership in the Context of Pastoral Leadership," *Christian Education Journal* 12 (autumn 1991): 49.
6. Vern Heidebrecht, "Affirming the Laity for Ministry," *Direction* 19 (fall 1990): 48–49.
7. Henri Nouwen, *The Wounded Healer* (Garden City, N.Y.: Image, 1979), 37–38.
8. Romans 2:8; 2 Corinthians 12:20; Galatians 5:20; Philippians 1:17; 2:3; James 3:14, 16.
9. Mihail Heller, *Cogs in the Wheel—The Formation of Soviet Man* (New York: Knops, 1988), 66–67.

10. Morton F. Rose, "Steps toward Servant Leadership," *Search* (spring 1990): 19.

11. Kenneth O. Gangel, "Biblical Theology of Leadership," *Christian Education Journal* 12 (autumn 1991): 30.

12. David Neer, "Leading the Liberated," *Issues and Observations* 16 (1996): 6.

13. John Greenleaf Whittier, "Dear Lord and Father of Mankind," the first and fourth stanzas of a hymn first published in *Horder's Congregational Hymns,* 1884.

CHAPTER 2—GIFTED PLAYERS—GIFTED COACHES: GIFTED LEADERSHIP

1. For a fuller treatment of biblical support of this concept see chapter three in my earlier work *Team Leadership in Christian Ministry* (Chicago: Moody, 1997).

2. A. Burge Troxel, "Accountability without Bondage: Shepherd Leadership in the Biblical Church," *Journal of Christian Education* 3 (spring 1982): 197.

CHAPTER 3—DESIGNING THE PLAYBOOK: CREATIVE ADMINISTRATION

1. John C. LaRue, Jr., "Time Management for Hard Working Pastors," *Your Church* (November/December 1998): 80.

2. Ibid.

3. Reba Rambo and Dony McQuire, *Wounded Soldier* (Nashville: Benson, 1985).

4. Howard G. Hendricks, *Color Outside the Lines,* Swindoll Leadership Library (Dallas: Word, 1998), 49.

CHAPTER 4—SETTING THE STANDARD FOR THE TEAM: LEADERSHIP MODELING

1. John Throop, "Be a Better Boss," *Your Church* (November/December 1998): 18.

CHAPTER 5—GETTING READY FOR THE GAME: EFFECTIVE FOLLOWERSHIP

1. Source unknown.
2. Robert Radcliffe, *Effective Ministry as an Associate Pastor* (Grand Rapids: Kregel, 1998), 91.

CHAPTER 6—KEEP YOUR EYE ON THE BALL: GOAL ACHIEVEMENT

1. Patrick Lenciono, *The Five Temptations of a CEO* (San Francisco: Jossey-Bass, 1998), 112.
2. This period of sixteen years is based on the fact that Aquila and Priscilla were expelled, along with all Jews, from Rome by the Roman emperor Claudius in A.D. 49 and the assumption that Paul was executed in A.D. 67.
3. Herb Miller, "Leading Indicators," *Leadership* (fall 1998): 79.
4. Caela Farren and Beverly L. Kaye, "New Skills for New Leadership Roles," in *The Leader of the Future,* ed. Frances Hesselbein, Marshall Goldsmith, and Richard Beckhard (San Francisco: Jossey-Bass, 1996): 187.
5. A. Richard Hackman, "Why Teams Don't Work," *Leader to Leader* (winter 1998): 30–31.
6. James M. Kouzes and Barry Z. Posner, "Seven Lessons for Leading the Voyage to the Future," in *The Leader of the Future,* 110.

CHAPTER 7—LOOKING DOWN THE FIELD: STRATEGIC PLANNING

1. Louis A. Allen, *The Management Profession* (New York: McGraw-Hill, 1964), 97.
2. Ibid.
3. John C. LaRue, Jr., "Pastors at Work: Where the Time Goes," *Your Church* (July/August 1998): 80.
4. Max De Pree, *Leading without Power* (San Francisco: Jossey-Bass, 1997), 117–18.

5. James F. Engle, "The Mission Board and the Local Church: It's an All-New Game," *Courier* 5 (summer 1996): 3.

6. Ibid.

7. Frances Hesselbein, "Journey to Transformation," *Leader to Leader* (winter 1998): 6.

8. Judith M. Bardwick, "Peacetime Management and Wartime Leadership," in *The Leader of the Future,* 134.

9. Hesselbein, "Journey to Transformation," 6.

10. Ibid., 7.

11. Robert K. Greenleaf, quoted in N. T. Fraker and Larry C. Spears, eds., *Seeker and Servant: Reflections on Religious Leadership (The Private Writings of Robert K. Greenleaf)* (San Francisco: Jossey-Bass, 1996), 54 (italics his).

CHAPTER 8—CHANGING THE GAME PLAN: INTENTIONAL INNOVATION

1. Peter F. Drucker, "The Shape of Things to Come," *Leader to Leader* (fall 1996): 17.

2. Peter M. Senge, "The Ecology of Leadership," *Leader to Leader* (fall 1996): 18.

3. Peter Koestenbaum, *Leadership: The Inner Side of Greatness* (San Francisco: Jossey-Bass, 1991), 308 (italics his).

4. Doug Murren, "The Leader as Change Agent," in *Leaders on Leadership,* ed. George Barna (Ventura, Calif.: Regal, 1997), 207.

5. Douglas J. Rumford, "The Art of the Start," *Leadership* (spring 1989): 85–86.

6. Douglas K. Smith, "Making Change Stick," *Leader to Leader* (fall 1996): 25–26 (italics his).

7. Dayton Fandray, "Re-defining Leadership," *Continental* (January 1999): 61 (italics his).

8. Price Pritchett and Ron Pound, *The Stress of Organizational Change* (Dallas: Pritchett and Associates, n.d.), 9.

CHAPTER 9—GIVE IT YOUR BEST:
QUALITY CONTROL

1. Peter M. Senge, "The Practice of Innovation," *Leader to Leader* (summer 1998): 17–18.

2. W. Edward Deming, quoted in R. I. Miller, *Applying the Deming Method to Higher Education* (Washington, D.C.: CUPA, 1991), 2.

3. W. Edward Deming, quoted in Mary Walton, *The Deming Management Method* (New York: Putnam, 1986), 72.

4. David A. Nadler and Mark B. Nadler, "The Success Syndrome," *Leader to Leader* (winter 1998): 49–50.

5. W. Edward Deming, quoted in Walton, *The Deming Management Method,* 78–79.

6. See my book *Ministering to Today's Adults,* Swindoll Leadership Library (Nashville: Word, 1999).

CHAPTER 10—AFTER THE STARTING GUN:
EMPOWERING OTHERS

1. C. William Pollard, "The Leader Who Serves," in *The Leader of the Future,* 246.

2. J. Donald Phillips, "What Do You Think about Your Delegation Practices?" *Hillsdale Report,* 12, no. 2 (n.d.): 5.

3. Pollard, "The Leader Who Serves," 244.

4. Doug Burrell, "The Forgotten Key to Effective Leadership," *Ministry* (May 1997): 27.

5. Olan Hendrix, "Managing Volunteers," *Hendrix Briefings* (April 1998): 3.

6. Alfred C. DeCrane, Jr., "A Constitutional Model of Leadership," in *The Leader of the Future,* 254.

7. Gifford Pinchot, "Creating Organizations with Many Leaders," in *The Leader of the Future,* 27.

8. Richard A. Kauffman, "Beyond Bake Sales," *Christianity Today,* 15 June 1997, 13.

9. Ibid. (italics his).

10. Peter Block, "The End of Leadership," *Leader to Leader* (winter 1997): 13.

11. Pollard, "The Leader Who Serves," 241.

CHAPTER 11—DESIGNING A CLIMATE-CONTROLLED GYMNASIUM: LEADERSHIP ATMOSPHERE

1. De Pree, *Leading without Power,* 105.

2. Ibid., 112.

3. Ron Klassen and John Koessler, *No Little Places* (Grand Rapids: Baker, 1996), 20–23.

4. Nadler and Nadler, "The Success Syndrome," 47.

5. John MacArthur, Jr., "How Shall We Then Worship?" in *The Coming Evangelical Crisis,* ed. John H. Armstrong (Chicago: Moody, 1996), 181.

6. Os Guinness, "Sounding Out the Idols of Church Growth," in *No God but God,* ed. Os Guinness and John Seel (Chicago: Moody, 1992), 155.

7. Raymond C. Ortlund, "Priorities for the Local Church," in *Vital Church Issues,* ed. Roy B. Zuck (Grand Rapids: Kregel, 1998), 91.

8. Stephen Covey, "The Habits of Effective Organizations," *Leader to Leader* (winter 1997): 22.

9. Ibid., 23.

10. U.S. Bureau of Labor, "The Real Meaning of On-The-Job Training," *Leader to Leader* (fall 1998): 61.

CHAPTER 12—DESIGNATED HITTERS AT BAT: CHURCH OFFICERS

1. C. Gene Wilkes, *Jesus on Leadership* (Wheaton, Ill.: Tyndale, 1998), 14.

2. Ibid., 191.

3. Fritz Rienecker, *A Linguistic Key to the Greek New Testament,* ed. Cleon L. Rogers, Jr. (Grand Rapids: Zondervan, 1980), 623.

4. Charles R. Swindoll, *Improving Your Serve* (Dallas: Word, 1981), 211.

5. Joseph M. Stowell, *Shepherding the Church* (Chicago: Moody, 1997), 148.

6. Paul wrote a brilliant statement on Christology in 1 Timothy 3:16. He said, "Beyond all question, the mystery of godliness is great," a reference to Christ. Then he touched briefly on the Incarnation, miracles performed by the Holy Spirit's power, angelology, evangelism, salvation by faith, and Christ's ascension and glorification.

CHAPTER 13—NO TRASH-TALKING IN THE HUDDLE: TEAM RELATIONSHIPS

1. Peter F. Drucker, *The Effective Executive* (New York: Harper & Row, 1967).

2. Pollard, "The Leader Who Serves," 247.

3. Steven M. Bornstein and Anthony F. Smith, "The Leader Who Serves," in *The Leader of the Future*, 283.

4. Thomas Gillmore, *Making a Leadership Change* (San Francisco: Jossey-Bass, 1988), 217–20.

5. Marshall Goldsmith, "Ask, Learn, Follow-up and Grow," in *The Leader of the Future*, 229.

6. Dave Ulrich, "Credibility X Capability," in *The Leader of the Future*, 212–13.

7. David Cormack, *Team Spirit* (Grand Rapids: Zondervan, 1989), 41.

8. William N. Plamondon, "Energy and Leadership," in *The Leader of the Future*, 275.

9. "From Team Member to Team Leader," *Team Management Briefings* (1998): 1.

10. The Greek word *homothymadon* is also used in Acts to describe the togetherness of those who opposed Stephen (Acts 7:57) and Paul (18:12; 19:29).

11. Margaret J. Wheatley and Myron Kellner-Rogers, "The Paradox and Promise of Community," in *The Community of the Future* (San Francisco: Jossey-Bass, 1998), 15.

CHAPTER 14—COACHING IS THE KEY:
TEAM PROCESS

1. Tom Phillips, "Building a Team to Get the Job Done," in *Leaders on Leadership,* ed. George Barna (Ventura, Calif.: Regal, 1997): 222.
2. Ibid., 226.
3. "Wanted: (Team) Leaders at All Levels," *Leader to Leader* (winter 1998): 53.
4. Larry Green, "Putting People in Their Place—Matching Ministers and Ministries," *Church Planter* (second quarter 1997), n.p.
5. Leighton Ford, "Helping Leaders Grow," in *Leaders on Leadership,* 145.
6. H. B. London, Jr., "Being a Tough but Tender Leader," in *Leaders on Leadership,* 112–13.
7. Jon R. Katzenbach, "Making Teams Work at the Top," *Leader to Leader* (winter 1998): 33–36.

CHAPTER 15—CHANGING TEAM CAPTAINS:
LEADERSHIP TRANSITION

1. Gangel, *Team Leadership in Christian Ministry,* 434–35.
2. Fred Smith, "Spotting a New Leader," *Leadership* (fall 1996): 31–33.
3. Olan Hendrix, "Starting Over," *Hendrix Briefings* (October 1998): 4.
4. "Seven Practices for Effective Leadership Development," *Leader to Leader* (spring 1998): 54.
5. Gillmore, *Making a Leadership Change.*
6. Robert W. Dingman, *In Search of a Leader* (West Lake Village, Calif.: Lakeside, 1989), 39.
7. Ibid., 67.
8. Frances Hesselbein, "The Challenge of Leadership Transition," *Leader to Leader* (fall 1997): 7.
9. John C. LaRue, Jr., "Forced Exits: Personal Effects," *Your Church* (November/December 1996): 65.
10. Dingman, *In Search of a Leader,* 100.
11. Erickson, "Transition in Leadership," 298.

12. J. Veronica Biggins, "Advice to Boards Involved in Chief Executive Searches: 'Step Back, Take a Deep Breath, and Take Stock,'" *Board Member* (July/August 1996): 6.

13. William Sanford LaSor, *Great Personalities of the Old Testament* (Westwood, N.J.: Revell, 1959): 69.

14. Erickson, "Transition in Leadership," 314.

15. Gillmore, *Making a Leadership Change,* 136.

16. Ibid., 144–45.

17. Ibid., 145.

BIBLIOGRAPHY

Allen, Louis A. *The Management Profession.* New York: McGraw-Hill Book Co., 1964.

Anthony, Michael J. *The Effective Church Board.* Grand Rapids: Baker Book House, 1993.

Barna, George, ed. *Leaders on Leadership.* Ventura, Calif.: Regal Books, 1997.

Bensimon, Estela M., Anna Neumann, and Robert Birnbaum. *Making Sense of Administrative Leadership.* Washington, D.C.: George Washington University, 1989.

Berkeley, James D., ed. *Leadership and Administration:* Leadership Handbooks of Practical Theology. Grand Rapids: Baker Books, 1994.

Cedar, Paul. *Strength in Servant Leadership.* Waco, Tex.: Word Books, 1987.

Clark, Kenneth E., and Miriam B. Clark. *Choosing to Lead.* Charlotte, N.C.: Leadership Press, 1994.

Cormack, David. *Team Spirit.* Grand Rapids: Zondervan Publishing House, 1989.

Covey, Stephen R. *Principle-Centered Leadership.* New York: Simon & Schuster Co., 1992.

De Pree, Max. *Leading without Power*. San Francisco: Jossey-Bass Publications, 1997.

Dingman, Robert W. *In Search of a Leader*. West Lake Village, Calif.: Lakeside Books, 1989.

Drucker, Peter F. *The Effective Executive*. New York: Harper & Row, 1997.

Enroth, Ron. *Churches That Abuse*. Grand Rapids: Zondervan Publishing House, 1992.

Finzel, Hans. *Empowered Leaders*. Swindoll Leadership Library. Nashville: Word Publishing, 1998.

Fisher, James C., and Kathleen M. Cole. *Leadership and Management of Volunteer Programs*. San Francisco: Jossey-Bass Publications, 1993.

Ford, Leighton. *Transforming Leadership*. Downers Grove, Ill.: InterVarsity Press, 1991.

Fraker, N. T., and Larry C. Spears, eds. *Seeker and Servant: Reflections on Religious Leadership (The Private Writings of Robert K. Greenleaf)*. San Francisco: Jossey-Bass Publications, 1996.

Gangel, Kenneth O. *Feeding and Leading*. Grand Rapids: Baker Book House, 1989.

_____. *Team Leadership in Christian Ministry*. Chicago: Moody Press, 1997.

_____, and Samuel L. Canine. *Communication and Conflict Management in Churches and Christian Organizations*. Nashville: Broadman Publishers, 1993.

Gillmore, Thomas N. *Making a Leadership Change*. San Francisco: Jossey-Bass Publications, 1988.

Habecker, Eugene. *Rediscovering the Soul of Leadership*. Wheaton, Ill.: Victor Books, 1996.

_____. *The Other Side of Leadership*. San Francisco: Jossey-Bass Publications, 1992.

Hesselbein, Frances, Marshall Goldsmith, Richard Beckard, and Richard F. Schubert, eds. *The Community of the Future.* San Francisco: Jossey-Bass Publications, 1998.

———, eds. *The Leader of the Future.* San Francisco: Jossey-Bass Publications, 1996.

———, eds. *The Organization of the Future.* San Francisco: Jossey-Bass Publications, 1997.

Johnson, Douglas W. *Empowering Lay Volunteers.* Creative Leadership Series. Nashville: Abingdon Press, 1991.

Klassen, Ron, and John Koessler. *No Little Places.* Grand Rapids: Baker Books, 1996.

Koestenbaum, Peter. *Leadership: The Inner Side of Greatness.* San Francsico: Jossey-Bass Publications, 1991.

Kotter, John P. *How Leadership Differs from Management.* New York: Free Press, 1990.

Kouzes, James S., and Barry Z. Posner. *Credibility: How Leaders Gain and Lose It, Why People Demand It.* San Francisco: Jossey-Bass Publications, 1993.

————. *The Leadership Challenge.* Rev. ed. San Francisco: Jossey-Bass Publications, 1995.

Levering, Robert. *A Great Place to Work.* New York: Random House, 1995.

Means, James E. *Leadership in Christian Ministry.* Grand Rapids: Baker Book House, 1989.

Robert Radcliffe. *Effective Ministry as an Associate Pastor.* Grand Rapids: Kregel Publications, 1998.

Ryrie, Charles C. *Nailing Down a Board: Serving Effectively on the Not-for-Profit Board.* Grand Rapids: Kregel Publications, 1999.

Schaller, Lyle E. *Getting Things Done.* Nashville: Abingdon Press, 1986.

Stowell, Joseph M. *Shepherding the Church.* Chicago: Moody Press, 1997.

Westing, Harold J. *Church Staff Handbook.* Rev. ed. Grand Rapids: Kregel Publications, 1997.

Williams, Dennis, and Kenneth O. Gangel. *Volunteers for Today's Church.* Grand Rapids: Baker Book House, 1993.

Wilkes, C. Gene. *Jesus on Leadership.* Wheaton, Ill.: Tyndale House Publishers, 1998.

SCRIPTURE INDEX

SUBJECT INDEX

The
Swindoll Leadership Library

ANGELS, SATAN AND DEMONS
Dr. Robert Lightner

The supernatural world gets a lot of attention these days in books, movies, and television series, but what does the Bible say about these other-worldly beings? Dr. Robert Lightner answers these questions with an in-depth look at the world of the "invisible" as expressed in Scripture.

THE CHURCH
Dr. Ed Hayes

In this indispensable guide, Dr. Ed Hayes explores the labyrinths of the church, delving into her history, doctrines, rituals, and resources to find out what it means to be the Body of Christ on earth. Both passionate and precise, this essential volume offers solid insights on worship, persecution, missions, and morality: a bold call to unity and renewal.

COLOR OUTSIDE THE LINES
Dr. Howard G. Hendricks

Just as the apostle Paul prodded early Christians "not to be conformed" to the world, Dr. Howard Hendricks vividly—and unexpectedly—extends that biblical theme and charges us to learn the art of living creatively, reflecting the image of the Creator rather than the culture.

EFFECTIVE CHURCH GROWTH STRATEGIES
Dr. Joseph Wall and Dr. Gene Getz

Effective Church Growth Strategies outlines the biblical foundations necessary for raising healthy churches. Wall and Getz examine the groundwork essential for church growth, qualities of biblically healthy churches, methods for planting a new church, and steps for numerical and spiritual growth. The authors' study of Scripture, history, and culture will spark a new vision for today's church leaders.

EFFECTIVE PASTORING
Dr. Bill Lawrence

In *Effective Pastoring,* Dr. Bill Lawrence examines what it means to be a pastor in the 21st century. Lawrence discusses often overlooked issues, writing transparently about the struggles of the pastor, the purpose and practice of servant leadership, and the roles and relationships crucial to pastoring. In doing so, he offers a revealing look beneath the "how to" to the "how to be" for pastors.

EMPOWERED LEADERS
Dr. Hans Finzel

What is leadership really about? The rewards, excitement, and exhilaration? Or the responsibilities, frustrations, and exhausting nights? Dr. Hans Finzel takes readers on a journey into the lives of the Bible's great leaders, unearthing powerful principles for effective leadership in any situation.

END TIMES
Dr. John F. Walvoord

Long regarded as one of the top prophecy experts, Dr. John F. Walvoord now explores world events in light of biblical prophecy. By examining all of the prophetic passages in the Bible, Walvoord clearly explains the mystery behind confusing verses and conflicting viewpoints. This is the definitive work on prophecy for Bible students.

THE FORGOTTEN BLESSING
Dr. Henry Holloman

For many Christians, the gift of God's grace is central to their faith. But another gift—sanctification—is often overlooked. *The Forgotten Blessing* clarifies this essential doctrine, showing us what it means to be set apart, and how the process of sanctification can forever change our relationship with God.

God
Dr. J. Carl Laney

With tenacity and clarity, Dr. J. Carl Laney makes it plain: it's not enough to know *about* God. We can know *God* better. This book presents a practical path to life-changing encounters with the goodness, greatness, and glory of our Creator.

The Holy Spirit
Dr. Robert Gromacki

In *The Holy Spirit*, Dr. Robert Gromacki examines the personality, deity, symbols, and gifts of the Holy Spirit, while recapping the ministry of the Spirit throughout the Old Testament, the Gospel Era, the life of Christ, the Book of Acts, and the lives of believers.

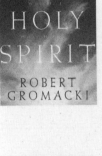

Humanity and Sin
Dr. Robert A. Pyne

Sin may seem like an outdated concept these days, but its consequences remain as destructive as ever. Dr. Robert A. Pyne takes a close look at humankind through the pages of Scripture and the lens of modern culture. As never before, readers will understand sin's overarching effect on creation and our world today.

Immanuel
Dr. John A. Witmer

Dr. John A. Witmer presents the almighty Son of God as a living, breathing, incarnate man. He shows us a full picture of the Christ in four distinct phases: the Son of God before He became man, the divine suffering man on Earth, the glorified and ascended Christ, and the reigning King today.

A LIFE OF PRAYER
Dr. Paul Cedar

Dr. Paul Cedar explores prayer through three primary concepts, showing us how to consider, cultivate, and continue a lifestyle of prayer. This volume helps readers recognize the unlimited potential and the awesome purpose of prayer.

MINISTERING TO TODAY'S ADULTS
Dr. Kenn Gangel

After 40 years of research and experience, Dr. Kenn Gangel knows what it takes to reach adults. In an easy-to-grasp, easy-to-apply style, Gangel offers proven systematic strategies for building dynamic adult ministries.

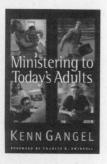

MORAL DILEMMAS
J. Kerby Anderson

Should biblically informed Christians be for or against capital punishment? How should we as Christians view abortion, euthanasia, genetic engineering, divorce, and technology? In this comprehensive, cutting-edge book, J. Kerby Anderson challenges us to thoughtfully analyze the dividing issues facing our age, while equipping believers to maneuver through the ethical and moral land mines of our times.

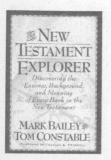

THE NEW TESTAMENT EXPLORER
Mark Bailey and Tom Constable

The New Testament Explorer provides a concise, on-target map for traveling through the New Testament. Mark Bailey and Tom Constable guide the reader paragraph by paragraph through the New Testament, providing an up-close-and-to-the-point examination of the leaders behind the page and the theological implications of the truths revealed. A great tool for teachers and pastors alike, this exploration tool comes equipped with outlines for further study, narrative discussion, and applicable truths for teaching and for living.

SALVATION
Earl D. Radmacher

God's ultimate gift to His children is salvation. In this volume, Earl Radmacher offers an in-depth look at the most fundamental element of the Christian faith. From defining the essentials of salvation to explaining the result of Christ's sacrifice, this book walks readers through the spiritual meaning, motives, application, and eternal result of God's work of salvation in our lives.

SPIRIT-FILLED TEACHING
Dr. Roy B. Zuck

Whether you teach a small Sunday school class or a standing-room-only crowd at a major university, the process of teaching can be demanding and draining. This lively book brings a new understanding of the Holy Spirit's essential role in teaching.

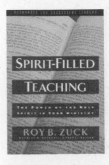

TALE OF THE TARDY OXCART AND 1501 OTHER STORIES
Dr. Charles R. Swindoll

In this rich volume, you'll have access to resourcing Dr. Charles Swindoll's favorite anecdotes on prayer or quotations for grief. In *The Tale of the Tardy Oxcart*, thousands of illustrations are arranged by subjects alphabetically for quick-and-easy access. A perfect resource for all pastors and speakers.

WOMEN AND THE CHURCH
Dr. Lucy Mabery-Foster

Women and the Church provides an overview of the historical, biblical, and cultural perspectives on the unique roles and gifts women bring to the church, while exploring what it takes to minister to women today. Important insight for any leader seeking to understand how to more effectively minister to women and build women's ministries in the local church.

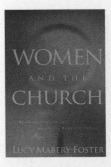